S E B R I N N E R   B L A I R

Forever, Jewels

Daily Essentials
for a Woman's Heart

authorHOUSE®

AuthorHouse™
1663 Liberty Drive
Bloomington, IN 47403
www.authorhouse.com
Phone: 1 (800) 839-8640

Published by AuthorHouse 10/26/2016

ISBN: 978-1-5246-4428-4 (sc)
ISBN: 978-1-5246-4426-0 (hc)
ISBN: 978-1-5246-4427-7 (e)

Library of Congress Control Number: 2016916784

Print information available on the last page.

This book is printed on acid-free paper.

Scripture quotations marked KJV are from the Holy Bible, King James Version (Authorized Version). First published in 1611. Quoted from the KJV Classic Reference Bible, Copyright © 1983 by The Zondervan Corporation.

Sebrinner Blair,

pastors at "Moving by the Word Ministries" in Daytona Bch. Fl.

THIS BOOK "FOREVER, JEWELS" IS PURPOSELY INTENDED TO ENCOURAGE US TO HAVE A BETTER DAY, ON PURPOSE!

These spiritual Jewels of wisdom, laughter, rest, peace, encouragement, and many more of our *Fathers* characters inside this book, will help us fight against depression, discouragement, anger, frustration and lack of confidence in self, and other negative forces that wants to overpower our lives.

Women... are you ready? Okay, let's go on this spiritual journey together and...

Worship, Laugh, Sing, Smile, Praise, Meditate, Reflect, and Interact...

"Forever, Jewels" will refresh your Spirit!

With:

Encouragement/Acceptance, Appreciation/Laughter

Self Assurance/Confidence, Rest/Relaxation

Peace/Quietness, Love/Joy and Worship!

This book is written with lots *of love, smiles, and prayers* for all of us to have a better and blessed life. *ENJOY!*

Dedication/Acknowledgements

What an honor, to dedicate **"Forever, Jewels"** to my **Heavenly Father**, who has inspired and instructed me to write this book, and for encouraging and carrying me through life's journey.

To Clarence Blair Sr. (husband) of 35 plus years, (Bishop & Sr. Pastor: Moving by the Word Ministries) my children, grandchildren, brothers, sisters, in-laws, and to "Moving By the Word Ministries Inc." church family.

If you are reading this book today, you are the reason and motivation for me writing this book of encouragement.

We all... need ENCOURAGEMENT!

As in a braid, there are 3 strands of hair moving in the same direction, so is their various ways of worship and meditation.

So, let's stay connected to our Heavenly Father....

And, "Put a smile on His face and keep one on ours." Smile!

Lastly, to all that has been in my life's path, thank you!

Introduction

This book **"Forever, Jewels"** is written to challenge every reader to stop, think, and search deep within themselves, to stay positive and overcome negative thoughts, *(whether you are a positive or a negative person)* that tries to weigh on us daily.

Forever, Jewels, is meant to encourage and lift our spirits to pull out the best that is already inside of us. This impartation of *"Positive Godly Character"* displays some of our *"Heavenly Fathers Character"* that He wants His children to possess. So, by having some of Gods qualities, *(even though all is better) we can continue to smile and appreciate life.*

This interactive book will help and enable us, to have a better and more productive spiritual life, and positive mind set to overcome the odds that will come against us in our daily lives.

"Please do not read this like a novel"

Please... Read, Laugh, Worship and INTERACT!

I hope and pray that this engaging and interactive book will lift your countenance, put *a smile on your face*, and bring joy to your soul!

Enjoy, God Bless!

Contents

FOREVER, JEWELS

Flowing Reflections from the Heart

I love thee oh Lord, with my whole heart, never leave me nor forsake me and I'll serve you until my end of days. *Selah*

Hear me oh Lord when I cry, Hear me oh Lord when I call on your majestic name. For you alone are worthy. *Teardrop*

Tears of joy let fall freely, let them cover the face of the earth. *Saturate*

Saturate my soul with your love *Holy Father.* My One True God, who has made all things beautiful in its time. *Forever Praise*

Heavenly Father, I will forever praise your eternal name. Your name gives life and your name gives hope. How wonderful is your name in all the earth. *Love*

Heavenly Father you are my precious jewel, a priceless gem, money can't buy! Thank you Jesus!!! You've always been my heart's desire so I'll always love you for who you are, and I'll never let you go. *Amen*

❖ *Look over there and get your jewel of compassion, see it?*

Whispering with your voice ever so softly through the night, whispering only to me what is right. Whisper to me when I'm over there, and when I'm going nowhere. And a whisper from my soul to yours I will declare. *Hear*

Heart to heart, hear me when I cry. From your heart to mine, my heart to yours. I really love you Jesus, I really, do! *Teardrop*

Drop down ye heavens from above, release your fresh anointing, rain on my soul, yes I am thirsty. Please fill my cup from above. *Selah*

Praise God, from above, oh my soul, praise God. Praise God for His everlasting love, praise God. God is love! *Worship*

Worship I owe, worship God, my mind! Worship God, my heart! Worship God, I must, all down in my soul!!! *Praise*

Open my eyes let me see. Open my ears let me hear. Open my heart dear Lord, and sup only with me. *Hungry*

Finding a position of rest and having a place of solitude. Oh Lord, dwell with me and I with you. *Meditate*

Meditating, on Gods' goodness and meditating, on Gods' holiness! Genuine and pure are you oh Lord, because your name is holy. *Remembrance*

❖ *A forever jewel of wisdom is coming your way, look for it today.*

Lord, I will remember your statutes because; they are forever resurfaced from inside my heart. *Teardrop*

Tears, tears, let them flow. Flow like a river and rejoice in the God of my salvation forever more. *Praise*

Praise the Lord, I will lift up my hands, I will sing and I will clap. For our God truly does reign! *Hallelujah*

Hallelujah, hallelujah, my God reigns! Hallelujah, hallelujah!!! Praise *God Almighty*, He reigns!!! *Eternity*

Eternal are you oh God, you are first and you are the last. You are the beginning with no end. Yes, you are the *Eternal God* forever and ever amen. *Forever*

Forever and ever I am yours! Forever and ever you are mine! Forever oh Lord, Forever. *Dedicated*

Dedicated, dedicated, dedicated, dedicated. Dedicated am I to you my Love. *Committed*

I am committed, committed to you. Commissioned to go and do. I am truly sold out to you. *Heart*

In my humbled heart I leap. I leap and leap till I can leap no more. *Joy*

Overwhelming, heavenly joy!!! Joy in the trees, joy in the leaves. So, let everything rejoice! And again I say rejoice! *Amen* From my heart to yours "I love you" and that's where it will forever start. *Rest my soul*

Leap and rejoice for the Lord God, our *Wonderful Savior* is with us. Praise the Lord everyone for He has come to comfort, and now my weary soul can rest. *Smile*

God smiles upon the righteous, and the righteous returns it back through obedience. *Laugh*

Wow!!! As I sit and watch the marvelous and wonderful acts of our *Creator*, laughter floods my happy little soul. *Selah*

Praise God for the marvelous! Praise God for the victorious! Praise God for all of His glory and holiness. Praise God my soul, praise God!!! *Reflections*

Reflect on Gods' mercy, Reflect on Gods' grace. Reflect on Gods' word and compassion, and His love forever more. *Forgiveness*

Forgiveness is of true value. Forgiveness, is it part of you? Please forgive your friend, your enemy and you. *Heart*

Cleanse my heart, oh God, clean deep inside my heart. Make me new, as a piece of your art. Yes! Lord, you are the potter and with my heart you can start. *Amen*

I would like to ask you something, how is your day? I pray that God make this day special for you and I really believe that He will. What do you think? Have a Wonderful Day!!! *Thoughtfulness*

Beauty's high, beauty's low, beauty's all around. Beauty's knocking at our door. Lord, we so desperately need your *Holy Spirit* to flow. *God*

God is here and God is there, God is so vast that He's everywhere. *Awe*

I stand in awe, as I see Gods' power released in the rain, lightning and the thunder. *Showers*

Surely, there's no time for guessing, because it's showers of blessings ready to release and set free its' wisdom and understanding. *Reign*

Reign over us take full control. Reign completely over my soul. Let your sweet *Holy Spirit* Reign. *Selah*

Free, free, free! Thank *God Almighty*; my soul has been set free! Praise the Lord, I'm free! And now I can finally see!!! *God*

When I see the lovely flowers, I see God. When I feel the refreshing breeze, I feel God. When I hear the birds singing, I then hear God. God is everywhere at all times if we can only see God! *Deep*

The bible say's "deep calleth unto deep". Can you hear the Lord calling you in your spirit? Is He calling you in your troubled times or is He calling you in your quiet times or both? *Teardrop*

Let God speak to our inner man. Let God speak to our spirit. Since, our spirit knows that we need God. *Heart*

Oh Lord, in my heart I will choose to love you. You only, will have the keys to my whole entire heart. *Desperation*

I live in desperation as my soul longs for your presence daily. For you, my *Heavenly Father* is my daily bread. *Teardrop*

Just as grass, trees, and fish in the sea cry for rain, Lord, as long as I live I will cry out for thee. *Hear*

Hear the frogs? Hear the crickets? I hear the Lord calling my name! *Selah*

Life seems long, but life is really short. Therefore, let us fear God and keep his commandments. *Fear*

I choose to fear God because I love God, and because I love God I chose to serve God. Now that's having the real fear of God. *Smile*

When God chose to save me, I saw Gods' goodness. Now, I can say with a smile along with a laugh that God is good! *Selah*

Praise is what I am, Praise is what I do. That's why I choose to praise God the Father and Jesus the son too. *Forever*

Praise God in the lowest valley, Praise God on the highest mountain. No matter where we're at let us stop and Praise Him, Praise Him, Praise Him!!!

Whenever I think of Jesus on the cross, I see His holiness in his face, hands and feet. So, I begin to cry and worship Him, now I can truly see. Yes, Jesus gave me a place to worship at His holy feet. *Deep*

When I look behind the clouds and I look beyond the heavens, I too, see Jesus looking back at me. *Smile*

Oh dear Lord, let us remember whenever we see the rainbow that it won't be water but fire next time. *Reflections*

Sign's are all around. Dogs barking, cats meowing, pigs oinking, ducks are quacking, sheep baaing, lions are roaring and birds are flying. Yes, the signs are all around. Didn't God speak through a donkey? *(Numbers 22: 28) Reflections*

Hallelujah!!! Hallelujah!!! Another day is here. The morning is come, the evening has gone, and the night has become no more. Hallelujah!!! For it's another day! *Selah*

❖ *Rest in the Lord, oh my soul!*

Do you hear what I hear? One beat, two beat, oh, it's a
heartbeat, life, life, life! Thank God for life!!! *Amazing*

So amazing are you to me, my dear Lord. Only you can heal the broken
hearted and save the lost soul. Lord, you are so amazing. *Thankful*

Thank you Lord, thank you! I just wanted to say "Thank you!" *Blessed*

You promised my Lord, that you would bless my seed. My seed,
my seed you promised that you would bless my seed. *Amen*

My lover my spouse, I am yours and you are mine, having
no surprise, because we're one in both eyes. *Love*

To be one in the night, sweet communion seems just right.
Meditating day and night, ready to take flight. *Passion*

Hold me close, hold me tight! Please do not let
me go my love for it is night. *Comfort*

I love thee oh Lord in the night watches, as I
meditate upon thy word. *Cleanse*

Cleanse me and don't let me stray. Cleanse my thoughts
and please, cleanse me from every evil way. *Grateful*

It is said, that weeping may endure for a night, but
joy comes in the morning. It is morning, it is morning!
Praise the Lord for it is morning!!! *Joy*

Joy, joy, joy!!! It's that unspeakable joy that floods my soul!
Yes, this heavenly joy from above, feel so good!!! *Dew*

As the morning dew, fall from heaven and covers the earth,
so will the love of God cover a multitude of faults. *Selah*

Just for whom you are, I will praise you. Because
you are God, that's who you are! *Teardrop*

Reflecting on God's goodness and reflecting on
God's grace... Lord, strengthen me to continue to
stay steadfast in this holy race. *Perseverance*

When I'm walking and running, shopping and sometimes going.
Oh Lord, help me to persevere as you keep on talking. *Conquer*

Are you a conqueror? Yes, I am a conqueror! I am more than a
Conqueror!!! I can do all things because you Lord, strengthens
me. I can jump mountains, I can speak to my situation by faith and
things change! Therefore, I am more than a conqueror. *Believe*

Release the right now blessing. It is now time for you Lord to
release the blessing. Surely I still believe it's on the way. *Promise*

Have you ever, sat and listened to the playful children? Out
of the mouth of babes, the Lord will perfect His praise. All we
have to do is take the time and listen to the children. *God*

We see beauty all around if we only just look around. Beauty's
in the air and it's in a stare. How dare we judge beauty from
without, when God made beauty from within, then out! *Beauty*

A quiet spirit and a quiet voice, that's when
God speaks without a doubt. *God*

Hush, hush, God is speaking! *Listen*

Have you read your bible sometime today? *Hear*

As calming waters quiet the soul, please listen
carefully and do not doze. *Selah*

Wow!!! I feel so good inside today. Why do I feel as though God l
me more than anyone else? Well, that's just the way He is. God mak
personal, now, doesn't it feel good to be loved! Have a lovely day! L

Give me more of you daily, Lord, give me more. *With love*

How wonderful to know that I'm not here alone as
your holy presence surround me. *Teardrop*

Living waters give me drink, I have eaten; now I must drink
and afterwards I will surely give you thanks. *(John 4: 7-15)*

A love, like no other! *Agape*

An unselfish and selfless love, you have Lord,
for the whole entire world. *Amazing*

One day, I will finally see your face. First time ever we will
really meet. In your loving strong arms, I will fall, forever
living with you and eternally happy after all. *Anticipation*

Here standing in line waiting. Waiting for my next assignment,
send me Lord! I'm now dressed and ready. *(Isaiah 8:1-8)*

Hallelujah!!! Hallelujah!!! To my king! The storms of life are passing
over and another sunshiny day is ahead. Hallelujah!!! *Thankful*

Remember the song, "Oh how I love Jesus, because He first
loved me?" The good news is, Jesus still does. He loves us more
than the song within itself, unconditionally!!! Why don't you try
singing the song, go ahead. I promise you'll feel better. *Love*

A lovely paradise of jewels may be hidden inside. Such as, fine jewels
of joy, peace, hope, love, gentleness, and meekness etc. We have it
in us but we must share it with the people in this world. If we choose
to let it come out, it will be a lovely paradise. *(Colossians 3:1-4)*

Like the smell of good brewed coffee or soothing chamomile tea, so is
the spirit of God running through my veins like the early morning dew.

Refresh

It's prayer time! It's prayer time! Make sure to make
quality time. It's definitely Prayer time!!! Let's stop
and pray before you go to the next line. *Cleanse*

Since you prayed, have you read your bible today? Why don't you
stop now, turn to (Psalms 51). Let's hear what God has to say.

Oh, I feel praise, I feel praise!!! I will not be ashamed of the
gospel! So, I will lift my hands and praise Him! *Selah*

My song for today is "I love thee Lord Jesus"
now that's my song. *Adoration*

Forever Lord will I sing to you. And forever my
dear Lord, you make my heart anew. *God*

Like having fresh oil and feeling the morning dew, is like expecting
Gods fresh anointing, created and designed just for you. *God*

I said to my soul, "Only worship God my soul!" *Selah*

I will pray for instruction, I will pray for direction. I will pray
for wisdom, knowledge, and understanding. *Selah*

Lord, please send your grace, and while you're at it,
give me your strength to run this race. *Endurance*

Holy Spirit, flood my soul because God only knows. *Trust*

I will trust in the Lord, my soul. I will trust in the Lord! *Faith*

When I think of my needs, and I think of God, I have no need. *Wholeness*

I was hungry and the Lord filled my cup, he proceeded on
and filled my plate. Thanks to God, I just ate. *Filled*

Upon my bed, I meditate and God saturates. *Teardrop*

To you only do I belong, my mind, heart, and soul, everything! *God*

God is giving out fruit today. Here, why don't you try gentleness. *Spirit*

Oh and while you're receiving gentleness, go ahead and get
some love, temperance, joy and peace. Yes, you will surely
need these today, while you're on your way. *Spirit*

Holy dreams as I lay my head. Surely, my God will
give me holy dreams. Rest he says, rest! *Selah*

Weeping may endure for a night, but remember
trouble don't last always. *Thankful*

I will keep my heart pure, I will. *Remembrance*

A trial will come, and this same old trial must go!
However, it did allow me to grow. *Thankfulness*

Yes!!! My heart is filled with gratitude and filled with praise. *Adoration*

To adore you is a must! To love you is a choice! And
with my choice you have added a plus. *Teardrop*

A new day has arrived. One generation has gone another generation
comes. Lord, I thank you for allowing me to see the sun. *Appreciation*

Press my soul, press! Again I say, that I must press! *Love*

Need strength to climb your mountain? Keep praying
and God will renew your strength! *Believe*

Peace, solitude, and, tranquility, hush not a sound. *Rest*
Never give up, never give up, I will not give up!!! *Hope*

Lord, you are a *Wonderful Savior, Wonderful God*! *Teardrop*

God you never changes, you are the same yesterday, today and forevermore. *Reflections*

Praise the Lord, for a home prepared and a home built. Heaven is the place we enter feeling no guilt. *Love*

Thank you Lord, for *Psalms 27* and *Psalms 23* because you've always been there for me. *Reflections*

I will love the Lord my God with all of my heart, soul, and all of my strength. *(Deuteronomy 6:5) Amen*

Trusting God for what we have is not trusting God at all. We must believe His word! *Faith*

Get away from it all. Get away my soul, get away my mind, pray, fast, and spend time with God! *Refresh*

Though, we have friends, children, family, jobs, and spouses, etc. There is a time we must have only (Jesus) steal away in quietness. *Love*

I will love Jesus, the lover of my soul. I will sing to Him a new song; meditate on Him, morning, noon and night, and love Him just right. *Emotion*

Dear Jesus, how I love you so, please whisper in my ear again and tell me something new. Refresh my spirit and make me more like you. *Teardrop*

Jesus did you call me today? Are you on your way? Just let me get prepared for your stay and its okay if you abide with me today. *Forever*

Always and forever, yes forever jeweled as stones are seen,
as they are placed inside a crown. So, if we were to see our
Heavenly Father's countenance it surely would not be a frown,
but is awesome in its entire splendor having great amazement
and beauty, He's *"King of Kings, and Lord of Lords."* Forever,
eternally crowned with majesty and honor, forever. *Beauty*

Flowing like springs of blue-green waters, free as a rainfall. These are
my tears of eternal love, flowing for my true and one-love. *Teardrop*

When you first opened mine eyes, it was truly love at first sight.
And with me...My *Love*, it was quite alright. *Forever Love*

Plain and simple "God" you are God! And that's just plain and simple....

I'm in love for the rest of my natural and eternal life, with
my Dear *Savior.* Yes, that feels quite nice.... *Smile!*

Lord, here I am, start again....I'm ready for another
one of your daily spiritual cleanse. *Pure*

❖ *My Promise Statement:*

I will treasure God more than silver or gold!

I will let the love of God flow through me for all to see!

I will pray to God in order to stay with God!

I will encourage, and tell myself that I am loved!

I will believe that I am beautiful!

I will think only on positive and uplifting things!

FOREVER, JEWELS

Growth

Even though you are reading this book today, have you read the bible today? Let God speak to you in a more direct and personal way.

Acceptable

Let the words of my mouth, and the meditation of my heart, be acceptable in thy sight, O LORD, my strength, and my redeemer. *(Psalms 19:14) KJV*

Emotions

Shedding tears aren't always bad. People cry *(tears of joy)* during weddings, when excited, and in times of sadness. Bottom line, tears show and express emotion. Jesus showed emotion when He laughed and wept, therefore, we should not allow our hearts to be so callous and hard. So, the next time God touch your heart, in what way will you show emotion?

Crave

Our bodies crave for water daily. Our body functions better with it than without it. How about a good cold glass of spring water Gods word and His spirit? Doesn't it feel good flowing in our warm dehydrated bodies?

Money

Thank God, we as believers trust in God and not in the value of the dollar. Doesn't that feel comforting to know? So, when stocks drop, our faith goes up! Hallelujah!!!

Expectancy

Have you ever seen the rain fall from the heavenly sky, when you did not expect it? Keep looking for an unexpected blessing today. Start thanking the good Lord for it now and the shower of blessings will begin to flow your way. When it come, just let it rain!

Refresh and Meditate

Yes Lord, (pause—slow deep breaths) repeat *(x10)*. Yes Lord, (pause—slow deep breaths) repeat *(x9)* with eyes closed, from the heart). Do it as needed. I hope and pray, this has helped your day. Be blessed!

A Promise

A promise is a promise, God doesn't lie. If God said it, He will do it. We must be patient, because with God a promise is a promise.

Question?

Okay, here's my question. Why do I choose to love you Lord? Answer: I don't know... I just choose too! That's my simple answer.

❖ *Possessing wisdom makes us love God more as the days go by. How sweet is that?*

Nothing But

Alright, can I just stop and praise the Lord of glory for a brief moment? I'll name it "Nothing, But Praise Break." *(LOL)* Come on, join in with me. You know that we all have a lot to praise God for.

A Light

In the dark and scary night, yes, there's light! When troubles come and friends seem to go, yes, there's light! When finances are at its low, here comes, light! Remember dear friend, there is always a light at the end of the road.

Forever, Letter

Hello, Jesus I know you're doing fine and all is well. I find myself thinking about you more each day. This is a short letter to say hello, my love. I must say that, the words that comes from your mouth to my heart, says that you are *holy in character, beautiful in splendor, and wonderful in every way.* With that in mind, I want you to know that you will always and forever be my one, true, first love, forever. Forever and a day, forever with my *Heavenly Father,* I will say, yes! This is my forever letter, and in my heart, dear God, I will hold you close. *Love*

Trusting

Trusting *God our Creator* for what we have is not trusting God at all. Remember, we must believe His eternal word! Now that's trusting God! *(Faith)*

Get Away

Get away from it all; get away my soul, away my mind.
Pray and fast, spend time with God the divine.

Quietness

Yes, we may have friends, family, jobs etc. However, there is a time
that we must only have (Jesus). What a wonderful opportunity to
seize and steal away in quietness, away from the crowd (a time to get
refreshed.) What we do in secret God will reward us openly. *(Saturate)*

Love Him

Love God the Almighty, the lover of our soul. Sing to Him a new
song; meditate on Him, morning, noon, and all throughout the
night. Constantly knowing, we must walk by faith and not by sight.
So if we continually love Him, our life will be bright. *Worship*

Who?

Meditations reflect our thoughts, thoughts can reflect our heart
and hearts can reflect who we really are. Who are you?

I Will

I will encourage myself today, tomorrow, and forever. Oh my soul, be
encouraged! Oh my soul you will be encouraged for God loves you!

Love God

Love God our *Eternal Savior,* because He is God. Love God for He gave His only begotten son, yes, Jesus gave His life for you. Love Him with all your mind, body, soul, and strength!

Everyday Quote

I am strong! I am rich! I am positive! I am encouraged!

A Moment

Thank you Lord! Thank you Lord! Repeat (x4)

I needed a moment to say thanks.

Listening

What must I do precious Lord, to love you more?
What must I do? I'm listening....

In Silence

When you're speaking to my heart in silence, it means more to me, than speaking to my ears aloud.

❖ *Believe in yourself and trust God to do the rest.*

Living

Loving God is to love life, and loving life is to look forward to spending eternity with the *Eternal God*. Now that's truly living....

Actions

Is to love God more than words? Yes, it must first come from the heart then expressed from the lips. So, go ahead and tell Him how much you really love Him, he'll be so glad you did.

Imperfections

Ever loved someone and you looked over all their flaws and imperfections? Give Jesus a try, he has none! And guess what, He won't judge you even if you have some. (Imperfections if I may say.)

Pause

To the one who is reading this, pause for a minute and let me ask you a question. How is your day? See how I thought of you... our *Holy* and *Eternal Father* thinks of us too. Now please do me a favor and enjoy the rest of this God-given day! *Xoxoxoxo*

Laugh

When is the last time you laughed? Try thinking of something that brought joy to you and begin to laugh. Laughter is like having a good dose of natural medicine. Now, don't you feel better? One more thing to remember, it's free and it's good for you. So, make sure you take it daily.

Rest

Question, when is the last time you rested? What part rested, if you know? Was it your mind, body etc. Well, the good news is that our *Heavenly Father* is waiting to give you the rest that you really need, please get your bible, turn to *Matthew: 11:28* and begin to read. You'll be so glad you did.

A Word

Listen, do you hear that? Quietness...Nothing! Now Lord God, speak to me for I have made myself available to you. Because I know in quietness..... God you still daily speaks to me.

?

Which direction? What shall I do? Have you ever asked those questions? Ask God even though you cannot physically see Him, God does hear you and He will tell you what you must do.

Sing

I will sing a new song unto the Lord and I will not worry about how I sound. I'm singing to my ...God! Hallelujah!!!

Planned Life

Heavenly Father, my life may seem to be a mystery to me, but you said "before I was born you had already planned the course for my life" Thank you *Father* for preplanning my future and I trust you with my life. *(Relationship)*

Forever, God

It's good to know, I have someone to come to. I have a *Father, Counselor, Savior, Comforter, Healer, Judge*, and so much more. Oh God, it's so good to know, you possess so many talents. You are God forever!

I'm Encouraged

I am blessed! I am highly favored! I am encouraged! Wow!!! I believe, I'll say that (x3) more times.

Know where you're going

Feeling a little confused or troubled? Listen, living in this world everyday is like living in a complete circle. But when we acknowledge God, He will lead us in a straight path. Praise God for stability! Hallelujah and Amen!

Just Say It

Utter His name, say His name and say it loud. Come on, don't be afraid, whisper it, He will hear you! Say it softly, come on just *say JESUS! (Meditate)*

Everlasting

To us there are seconds, minutes, and hours. To us there are days, weeks, months, and years. To us there's an end, but to God, He is! He is time, without end! Yes!!! God is eternity forever and ever, where there's no sin. Praise the Lord!!! *(Anticipation)*

It's Free

With all the worlds technology today there's a price tag on it. No need to worry, our *Heavenly Father* has given us a powerful tool, an open line of communication and it's totally free. Have you prayed today?

The Flesh

Ever been offended and wanted to give the so-called offender a piece of your mind? First, let's pray, then think twice and pray some more, because the last thing we want is to let our flesh speak! *(Wisdom)*

Enjoy

Here's a letter stamped with lots of love along with a bouquet of fresh flowers just for you, with a little twist (spray) of your favorite perfume, enjoy them! You deserve this and so much more. Have a blessed day. *(Thoughtfulness)*

The Right Thing

Loving God is always right, choosing not to love God is always wrong. Have you considered making the right choice today? Just thought I should ask.

❖ *Lord, I'm your jewel still in the making, and that's good to know.*

Mothering

Having been born in this earthly and physical realm, some women are fruitful in having children; some are not and even barren. But, thank God when we operate in the spiritual realm, we can all be fruitful in bearing seed (patient, kind, loving, etc.) because we are a God fearing woman. I AM A WOMAN! *(Character)*

Union Defined

Question, are you single, married, widowed or divorced? Well, it really doesn't matter because God say's, He has enough love for us all. We are forever joined together as one, so now, let the bride and groom say amen!

Think!

Being effective is not how much you do or how much you say. Think about it and let Gods character, speak!

Beauty

Colors in the rainbow are beautiful, and with our eyes we can see its variety. Also colors are different and unique since they can come in multiple shades and colors. Now aren't you happy God made you? *(Acceptance)*

❖ Please… Don't worry, give it to Jesus. He will work it out for you!

It's, There

Love, love is in the air, you can't touch it nor can you see it. But it really is there. Love is given to us from our *Heavenly Father* to share.

A Painting in the Sky

Have you ever seen the yellow sun standing still in the blue revolving sky in the day? What about the gray moon surrounded by the glistening stars in the night? Wow! Isn't it beautiful? Everyday day God, our *Creator* has given us a beautiful painting in the sky. *(Appreciation)*

Inside

Where is beauty? Do I look far or do I look near? Do I look here or there? No, Look no farther.... God says beauty has always started in the heart, look there.

Sweeten It

Lemons are not bad. So, if your attitude is more like a lemon, did you add your sugar today? Everyone can use a little sweetness even you! *(Heart)*

It's Feeding Time

Eating is something we must all do to survive. Now, with that thought in mind, did you eat your bread of life today? Yes, the B.I.B.L.E.

❖ *Aren't you lovely! Now, go ahead and smile!*

I Can

Never say you're too old; never say you're too young. Just
say and repeat this, I can do all things through Christ who
gives me strength. Now isn't that encouraging?

To Serve

The role of a leader is never about dictating or telling people
what to do. But the role of a leader is about serving. Since,
we have various titles, whether you are a mother, friend,
sister, etc. Whom have you chosen to serve today?

Do You Know?

Your name has been called; God has called for you to
go higher and deeper. Let me ask you a question if
you know, how deep is your roots in Christ?

For You

Today is a very special day! It's a day for you to feel extremely special.
So, please take this bouquet of red roses (allergic free) with you all day.
If you carry them in your heart, they will never depart. Love, God

❖　I love who I am, really…… I do!

Do It Again

Hush, God is speaking while you listen. Did you pray
or read your bible today? If so, what did He say, or do
you need to go back and pray? Just do it again.

Joy

No words have uttered from my lips, only from my heart and
now my heart Lord is flooded over with joy in abundance!

Relax

Do you like relaxing, drinking a good cup of coffee or tea early
in the morning before your day gets started? Go ahead and
while you're at it how about reading the bible too. *(Devotion)*

Praise Break Repeat (x4)

Praise break! Praise break! Here is my praise.
Hallelujah, thank you Jesus!!! (x4)

Lord *God Almighty*, I will praise and serve you for the rest of my life.

Mirror

Heavenly Father, when you look at me, please tell me
what you see? What do you see when you stare into
my soul? Am I a mirrored reflection of you?

Be Encouraged

There's something we want and something that we all need. We may never ask for it, but we surely need it. ENCOURAGEMENT!

Trivia

Is love really between two people, or do love start first in us? The answer is above, start with the first. Did you get it?

Pray

Warriors! Warriors! Calling all prayer warriors...Let's pray for the young men, they are made in the image of God our *Father*. Remember the saying "Like *Father*, like son?" Let us continue to pray.

Bride

The bridegroom is coming! The bridegroom is coming! Yes, we are the bride and we must be ready to meet Him (Jesus.) We have heard it over and over that one day the bridegroom is really coming. Let's be ready!

Acceptance

I was told that I was born on the other side of the tracks. Which side were you born on or does it really matter? With God it doesn't.

King!

Our *Eternal KING! Our Shepherd King,* no I did not say, Lord of the Rings. But, *"Lord of Lord's and King of King's"* yes, that's who He really is. Hallelujah, Hallelujah and Amen to our KING!!! *(God)*

His Grace

Long suffering, have you tried that fruit lately?
When you start eating that fruit, God say's

His grace is sufficient...

Looking Pretty?

As a woman, we like pretty things. We like pretty clothes, shoes, purses and even "The Perfect Family." However, in reality our life isn't always pretty. Trials will come and that's when we must allow God our *Creator* to cut out those ugly things from our life that comes only to hinder or completely stop us from serving our Heavenly Father to our fullest. When that is done, then our attitude will reflect the pretty things that God has already placed inside us all! We are the bride of Christ, now stay beautiful!

Jealousy

Jealousy is a terrible person, she seeks to envy someone better, wealthier, prettier and more popular and the list goes on and on. Now, listen very carefully...If this person comes knocking at your door, "Please! Please Don't Let Her In!" Let's continue to guard our hearts daily.

❖ *Loving our Heavenly Father above is what I choose to do for the rest of my life...*

Enjoy Life

A lemon is a sour fruit, but it can be sweetened, and a cucumber can be pickled. Our *Heavenly Father* has given us one life with a choice. We can choose to have it sweet, sour, or both. Which one will you choose? Enjoy your life today because this day will never come again. We don't have to live a bitter life; although, we do have a choice to sweeten it? Stay sweet!

Moment of Thanks

Let's take a moment to thank God for all the little and big things that he has happily done for us in our lives. 1 minute...2 minutes, go ahead and open your mouth. Let me help you, say Thank you Jesus! Thank you for peace! Thank you Jesus! Thank you for loving me! Thank you Jesus! Now you finish...Thank you Jesus for....

Grab It!

Children are a blessing...whether you are or have been fruitful or barren physically, it really doesn't matter. We can all experience walking in the spiritual blessings of God, since we are the children of God. What belongs to God belongs to us!!! So ...Claim it and grab it!

Prayer

Prayer is a wonderful line of communication; it needs no wires or batteries, neither does it use data or minutes. Prayer can never be lost because it's deep within our heart. As long as we use this free valuable resource that our dear *Heavenly Father* has given us, we're sure to never feel fatherless. Question, have you used your phone yet, because your *Heavenly Father* wants to hear from you? Oh! The good news is that there is no static in the line, so your call will be very clear. So, go ahead and start now.

A Day

There is a day just beginning – a day well spent, and a day of reflections. There is a day to look ahead and a day to seize every moment. However, another day will be coming, God willing.

Self

Here is something to think about. How do you see drug addicts? How do you see adulterers? How do you see strippers? Lastly, this a hard one, how do you see yourself? Are we really that much better or do we need a *Savior* and lots of prayer too? *(Luke 18:10)*

Grace

Athletes and actors are sometimes chosen because they are good at what they do. Are we really that good, that God chose us, or is it God's grace? Remember, let's not allow our titles and achievements fool us! It's only by Gods grace that we are who we are in Christ. Now that's truly amazing! *(Smile)*

When We

When we acknowledge the Lord throughout the day, what a wonderful, wonderful day need I say!

Like God

To hear God is to learn of God, to learn of God is want to see God. To see God is to want to be with God, and to be with God is to want to live with God. Yes! To live with God is the real reason we choose to live like God.

Flow

Since Jesus came into my life...flowing from my heart is abundance. Flowing from my heart is like a river, a river of life filled with eternal joy. Yes! Since Jesus came into my life....

Simple Poem

I wrote a simple poem for you today and I hope you like it. God loves you, yes you! *Reader,* God say's that He has always loved you! You are the apple of His eye, you are special. You, *dear reader* are cherished everyday and on His mind every day. Dearly beloved, only listen to His say and He will direct you in every way.

Healed

I am healed, I am healed. In my spirit and in my mind I am healed. In my body and soul I am healed. Thank *God Almighty* through faith and by His stripes I am completely healed.

Godly Expressions

Finding ways to express our love to God and people is a beautiful thing. Therefore, by reading our bible, praying and meditating, or helping someone in their time of need, always shows acts of love and kindness. Choosing to do right over wrong is also a godly act. So, when we fellowship with the saints, give of our finances to help spread the gospel of Jesus Christ, feeding the hungry, or working in the church, even giving words of encouragement are always expressions of love. Let's continue to do well, for in doing good God is well pleased.

Letting It Flow

In my life I will never be the same, I have been eternally changed! Yes, I am experiencing the joy of the Lord and what marvelous wonders, since Jesus came into my life. Now I will forever let his *Holy Spirit* flow ever so freely in my soul... *Jesus* let it flow....

Have a Moment

Do you have a quick moment? This won't take very long, a moment to tell our *Almighty God*, thank you! Come on and say with your mouth, Thank You Jesus! Come on and pull it out... say it again, Thank you Jesus! Thank you Jesus! Thank you Jesus! Thank you Jesus! Now that wasn't so hard, was it?

Forgive

So they did you wrong, you've been lied on and abused, lost friends and family too, or your spouse may have left you. While there are so many reasons to carry the hurt and pain, there's still no excuse. Carrying unforgiveness in our heart hurts and it wants to give us an excuse to not forgive. But we must forgive! Weep hard; cry loud, yes it hurts...its ok to let it go! You have carried pain long enough. My child, my child, "Forgive and Let it Go" says the Lord.

The Tempter

This person seems to come around every time we decide to do right. This person comes right by our side and tells us to do the complete opposite! We don't have to listen to its voice; this evil spirit means us no good. We must tell it to leave in Jesus name! Be bold, be brave, and be very courageous!!! Remember what *(James 4:7) KJV* says," Resist the devil and he will flee from you."

Born

I was born to worship and born to serve. I was born to worship and born to love. I was born to love, serve and worship. This is my purpose as I give myself wholly to Gods service, and I will forever cherish this wise little nugget.

Not a Dime

In this world, we have kings, queens and presidents, and we know them only by name. But thank God, we have a king that knows us and we can know Him. This king has given us an invitation into His kingdom, which has been prepared, designed, and well built, "New Jerusalem." This new home is prepared just for us, debt free, and no cost to us. How can this be? Well, the price was paid way back on Calvary. Hallelujah and Amen!!!

Praise

Have you ever heard a song or someone say, "I got a praise, I got a praise and I gotta let it out, I got a praise?" Well, let's go ahead and do a *(Psalms 150:2)*, Praise Him for His mighty acts: praise Him according to his excellent greatness. Let's praise the good Lord because He is truly worthy of our praise, praise is part of who we are as saints of God. Yes, as long as we have life we should be glad to praise the good Lord above. PRAISE HIM!!!

I Speak

I speak peace and joy in my soul, mind, and body. I speak peace! I speak joy! In Jesus name, amen!

Worship

Let us worship the *Father!* Let us worship the *Son!* Let us worship them as one! Let us Praise Him... Oh, let us praise Him to the highest mountain... Oh, let us praise Him in the lowest valley. Whatever state we are in, we are encouraged to press into the presence of the *Holy of Holies* and begin to freely worship having no restraints. Yes, this is the place where our *Heavenly Father* truly wants us to be, STRESS FREE! Dear Jesus, let it be for this is a privileged place for all to be. So here in your presence my Lord, I come to worship!

Challenge

Some risks are scary they can challenge us to go beyond our comfort zones. But this risk is worth taking, since we have nothing to lose. Are you ready? Here it is....Love the Lord thy God with all thy heart, and with all thy soul and with all thy mind, and with all thy strength: this is the first commandment. *(Mark: 12:30) KJV*

The Church

Have you ever been asked, what church do you go to, or what's the name of your church, or they may have asked what the name of your pastor is? With that said, we must never forget, we are the church, a host of believers who assembles in one place to worship the *"I Am that I Am, the One True Living God,"* Jesus Christ the Chief Shepherd of our souls. Let the church say AMEN to that!

Eat It

I hope you had your delicious and tasty fruit today. Be honest if you didn't, let's go on isle *(5:22-25 of Galatians.)* When you get it, go ahead and eat it. Why? This kind of fruit has all the right nutrients in it for us to spiritually survive and it's 100% good for the natural body. *(Smile!)*

Valuable

Gold and silver is an extremely valuable resource. We give it to department stores, family, friends, car lots, and grocery stores sometimes with regrets. But we must be very careful to whom we choose to give our soul.

Door

Doors keep things in and doors keep things out. Let us make sure that we are not keeping in what should be kept out! And let's not keep out what God is trying to put in. Can I hear a Hallelujah and amen?

Be Different

As I walked around the corner I saw lots of people, one was angry and bitter and started fighting. Another one was drunk and he got arrested, now turn to *(Galatians 5: 19-21)* and finish reading. Those of us that have received salvation through the cross of Christ, and have chosen to be different by living like Christ, if we continue to be an example to the unbelievers maybe just maybe, they will listen and choose to be different too.

Know

Where and what is beauty? Beauty looks like a flower before it blooms. Beauty sounds like music coming from a room. Beauty smells like someone's favorite perfume. Beauty can taste like fresh baked macaroons. Beauty is everywhere, it's in the air, it's unique and never the same. You are beautiful! Yes beautiful, however one must first know that it is there. BEAUTY!

Just for You

Everyone likes flowers or gifts every now and then. So why wait for someone to bring them to you? Go get them for yourself and enjoy your day. What you do for you matters too. Treat yourself sometime.

Looking

Because you are reading this right now, I believe that you are searching or looking for a word of encouragement. Let me speak into your life (spirit) right now. Be not weary in well doing. Keep trusting and believing God. Keep praying and looking to God our *Father*, and He will supply your need. Lastly, Do Not Be Discouraged since God is for us, and in Him we should trust.

Free

Have you heard about the free gift in *(Acts 2:38?)* Check it out and don't forget to tell others about. Let's spread the good news of Jesus Christ. Oh yes, and remember to tell them that it's free. Hallelujah!!!

Change

Can I speak a word of transformation over your life? As a caterpillar that transforms into a beautiful butterfly change can be a beautiful thing, only when we accept it. We must not be afraid to shed off the old in order to become that new creature that our creator has created us to be. Look at it this way, *God the Creator* had started work on us inside of our mother's womb before we came into existence, for everyone to see. I speak change over your life, you will be fruitful and not barren, and you will have more hunger for the things of God. You also will have a sound mind. Now, continue to let the potter transform you into His holy image? *(Romans 12)* is a good place to start, God bless.

We Can't

Choosing to love God more than ourselves, how,
can we go wrong? Answer, we can't.

Gossip

Did you hear about what happened to your neighbors down the street?
Gossiping! Let's be honest, we love to talk... but gossip is just like the
wind it comes smooth but does very destructive damage in the end.
Lord, have mercy on us and we pray your forgiveness you would send.

Married?

Married, never been married, don't want to be married, divorced,
or widowed? There is a special day coming when the *Bridegroom*
is coming back for His bride (the church). We are the bride if we
choose to follow and be one with God spiritually. So, let us keep
our gowns on and clean, waiting for our big day. Please, please
don't throw your gown away. Remember, Christ did say that He
would come back real soon and take us away. Yes, take us away!

Faith or Fear

What will I choose when I don't have enough, or I don't see my way out?
Will I choose to walk in fear or will I choose to walk in faith? Well, let me
think for a minute, Fear is not trusting God and faith is trusting in God
completely. Well, here's my answer...I choose FAITH! What about you?

Only You!

Only you oh Lord is worthy of my praise! Only you is worthy of my sacrifice. Only you oh Lord, stand in an arena having no competitors. You can never be second, third or fourth, because you are first. God the beginning, God the end! God the first and God the last! Only you my Lord stand in a category alone.

Felt Like?

Ever had a stressed out emotional week or longer? Or was it a couple of weeks? Example, I was sitting alone after a long, tired, and draining couple of weeks, that I said "I feel like complaining and I feel like being sad" with tears about to fall. But right in the midst... I decided to Praise God instead... and it felt so... good and refreshing.

It's, Here!

My time and season is here. I see it Lord, I see it now! I see it from afar and I see it near. I will embrace it and I will walk in it! Yes, my time and season is truly here....

What is Faith?

What is faith? Faith is something not physical or tangible; faith believes God at his word. Remember this saying "If God said it that settles it!" Well my friend, just say it now! I believe what our *Heavenly Father* has spoken in my life, yes, I am blessed... yes, I am the head and not the tail... yes, I am in my right mind... and yes, God is on my side! Yes, I am highly favored of the Lord!!! Now that's faith in action.

What Joy!

Leap Jesus... leap John! I leap and I leap for the good news
has come! So, I leap and leap, and leap some more. Oh, what
everlasting joy... Leap my soul, leap and then leap some more!

Dream

Have you ever dreamed? If you haven't or you don't remember, ask God
to refresh your dreams... Please do me a favor and keep your dreams
alive. Keep imagining and keep dreaming about something bigger than
you. Keep your dreams alive, because dreams really do come true.

Valley to Mountain

When you were in your valley low, I was there. I guided and
protected you, it was I the Lord your God. When you came
through the valley and climbed the mountain, I strengthened
your legs and held you steady;. I knew you were ready, so
remember it is the Lord your God as you go to the next level.

Say, I Believe

Faith, activate! I believe and trust you my Lord.

I believe and trust you my Lord. I believe and trust you my Lord.

Now, keep repeating it until you believe what you are
saying and your faith is continually activated!!!

Daily Choice

Born to know God and called to serve God. But, I also choose to love God. Wow!!! What a choice! What a choice! What a daily choice!

Heavens Scent

Ever wondered how heaven smell, or how we smell to heaven? Everyday there are billions and zillions of saints prayers that are perfuming heaven daily. If we are included in the number above, God in return pours back into us a sweet aroma of his heavenly spirit.... So, when we are kind, compassionate, understanding, and tender-hearted, etc. we send a smell of our *Heavenly Fathers* presence here on earth. Then all people will experience heavens scent as we the children of God represent.

Day to Pray

A day to pray... Today I pray for... (Fill in) and.... (Fill in) my family, friends, and my enemies (known and unknown) too. Bless them today Lord and last but not least, bless me. This is my prayer today, in Jesus holy and mighty name, amen!

I Am

Who am I? Am I what I feel? Am I what I have been through? No! I am fearfully and wonderfully made in the image of God, my *Heavenly Father*. That's who I am! Because this statement is so true, I must repeat this a second time. Hallelujah!!!

Flower

Here is a flower just for you today. Do you see it? Imagine
your favorite flower, now touch it, feel it, smell it, and
observe it! You deserve it, carry it...A spiritual flower
just for you! Now enjoy and have a blessed day!

Love Yourself

I love me, I love myself. I love who I am. I love the flawed me
and I love the strong part of me. Why? Because God loves me!
I love my hands, my eyes, and my smile. I love my hair, my legs
even my backside (laugh out loud!)Yes! Every part of us we must
love. Thank you *Jesus* for making me who I am! *(Appreciate)*

Beautiful Day

Today is a beautiful day! What a beautiful day! Oh, it's just a gorgeous
day or should I say a wonderful day? Well, it's just a beautiful, beautiful
day!!! Now enjoy it! (Before a day begin, always remember we must
speak it). Because if we don't speak for ourselves, who will?

At The Table

My soul is so excited today, because our *King*, our *Savior* has come to
sup with us today. We're having bread and water and He is serving
us at the table. Yes, and I am enjoying every single moment with
Him. I hope you are enjoying Him too! Can you really believe that
our *King* is really here communing with us at the table? Believe it!

Closer

Hold me a little closer to you Lord. Embrace me a little bit
tighter. Comfort me with your *Holy Spirit* and let me forever
be warmed with your loving arms. And Lord never, never,
let me go and with you one day I will eternally go.

Cool Waters

Blue waters, cool waters, refreshing waters! Oh yes, it's the
living waters that I feel deep within my thirsty soul!

LOL

Can you please take a moment and think of someone or something
that made you laugh? Do you remember it? Go ahead and think
about it, enjoy that special moment again and laugh out loud!
Hey, laughter is good so make sure you do it often. Life isn't that
bad that you can't laugh... The bible say's weeping may endure
for a night but joy will come in the morning. Laughter works
like medicine so make sure you take it daily. Now LAUGH!!!

Take a Moment

A moment of solitude, yes take a moment please. A moment
of stillness, (quietness) go ahead and take a moment to wind
down. It's really okay for you to just take a "me moment"
because in the beginning "Genesis" God took a whole day!

❖ *What good is it, if we love everyone else and don't love ourselves*

Daily Cleanse

Lord, I bring true praise from the heart along with true worship
right from the start. A meek and quiet spirit from within,
here I am again Lord, seeking you daily to depart from sin.
Knowing this is not the end, since this is my daily cleanse.

Peaceful Time

Peace is in the air. A peaceful time is lingering near. I feel
it and I receive it! Peace is singing a very sweet lullaby in
my ear. Thank God for His holy peace, it's here!

My Soul, I will love God, oh my soul! I will praise God, oh my soul!
I will serve God, oh my soul! So take heed my soul, take heed!

If Ever

If ever I forget to say "I love you," I love you! If ever I forget to say,
"Thank you," Thank you! If ever I forget to show you that I care, "I care."
If ever I forget to say I'm sorry, "I'm sorry!" Lord, always remember
and never forget, "I will always love you, forever and ever..."

Peace

Thank you Lord! Thank you for giving me this special day
to saturate. Saturate me with your divine peace. Peace you
have spoken and peace I receive. So, I thank you today *Holy
and Eternal Father* for your God-given peace. Some say peace
out, but I say thank you God for your peace within.

Blessed!

Blessed art thou oh Lord. Merciful art thou oh Lord. Forever art thou oh Lord, forever thou will be my God! Truly my God is forever blessed!

Clean & Pure

A clean heart, a clean heart! A clean heart, oh God!
Lord, I just want a clean and pure heart!!!

Therapy

Spiritual therapy is what we need. We get fractured and wounded. We get broken and scarred. Oh, by the way, have you prayed today? Did you take your relaxer meds today to calm those over worked muscles and nerves? How about applying the word of God over your body from head to toe? Go ahead, it's not too late. Dr. Jesus has already written the prescription that you need. So, take as much as you want, I guarantee, you won't overdose on this, you will live and have life more abundantly. Please make time to read and study the "Word of God" and please don't forget to pray along the way. We all can use this kind of spiritual therapy. Don't you agree?

Hush...Listen....

Hush...Hush... Do you hear that? Maybe God is trying to tell you something... Keep listening. You don't have to say anything, just keep listening....Hush! God is trying to say something. In the book of James, James advice is to be quick to hear and slow to speak. Now listen....

Just God

I never knew someone could love me the way you do.
You have shown it and you continue to prove it daily.
Because that's just who you are God, that's just you!

The Power

One heart...One mind, one body...One life! One God and
one *Father* above all! Truly that's the power of the spiritual
#1 (ONE). Without the number one *(God)* there is no other
number. Without A *(Alpha)* there is no B, C, or D...Yes! There
is *NO POWER* above our God! Now, that's POWERFUL!!!

❖   *Love God! Love God! Love God...I Will!*

Questions

Have you ever had more questions than answers? For instance, what's my purpose? Why was I born? Why did I have to go through this and why did I have to go through that? Well... Some of your questions will be answered but unfortunately, some will never be answered. But do you remember the old saying, "Baby...by and by... you will understand it by and by."

So, I will say to you today, be encouraged and be not weary while working for the Lord. Continue to let your light shine because questions will always be a part of our lives, and hopefully one day we will understand *some things* as they say, by and by. Let's do that and let the good Lord do the rest? *(Smile)*

Let It Rain

Have you ever been hoping and praying for fresh rain? Rain so fresh, that it washed all of your worries away, all because it was a spiritual rain. Yes, you are wet and even washed, but your outer garment has not been touched. God is doing an inner cleansing of the mind, body, spirit and soul. Now continue to meditate on the Lord, because the process has already begun. Let God shower His heavenly blessings in your thirsty soul.

Wondered

Tell me this, have you ever wondered, how can you love someone that you have only heard of? Or, how can someone live again that died over two thousand years ago? Answer: FAITH! Without faith it is impossible to please God, but all things are possible to him that believeth...FAITH!!!

Commune

Lover of my soul.....Commune with my heart... Lover of my
soul! Lover of my soul...Come commune with your spouse!
Lover of my soul... Lover of my soul... Lover of my soul....
Lover of my only soul! To commune with you I owe....

New

I am a new creature renewed by God the Creator.
Old things have passed away, and what more can I
say but to give God thanks for this new day.

<u>Another Reflection</u>

You love me...You love me. You love me... Forever and always
you will love me. My Lord does truly love me! *Assurance*

Blessed assurance is a song that say's Jesus is mine, on my mind
is Jesus as I sit and think, morning, noon and night. *Peace*

Surrounding me is the purest of pure. Surrounding me
is the holy of holies. Surrounding me is the great I am!
Surrounding me...Surrounding me! *Surrender*

Oh Lord my God, my *Savior*. I yield my will over to you. I confess and
repent. I surrender and completely give myself wholly to you! *Teardrop*

My Lord, you are my Lord. I will serve you. I will love you. I am yours and
you are mine. My Lord! My Lord! For we are one my Lord, one! *Bride*

The love of my life, always have and always will be now till eternity! *Love*

Fix My Heart

As I listen only to you I give you my heart, Here it is Lord, take it, you can have it...it may be a little broken. You may find a crack here and there, but I believe that you can fix it better than it was before. I heard that you are a *great and skilled carpenter, an excellent potter, masterful genius, creative artist, doctor, lawyer, realtor,* and you have heavenly degrees in every known and unknown field of expertise. So, with all that wisdom, knowledge and understanding, please fix my heart Lord, I trust you!

Passion

What??? What is it? Why do I feel a burning down on the inside of me? It's a fire of passion...called to it and chosen for it! Gods' holy will... That's what! It's my purpose that I must fulfill....PASSION!

All My Life

My love, how marvelous and wonderful is you in my eyes.
I searched to know you all my life from my youth, and now
I have found you. Now I will not let you go! My love beauty
is you; yes you are the apple of mine eye! *(Love)*

Your, Bride!

A letter to my dearly beloved, even though you seem so far away, yet I know you're so very close. In my heart you are the love of my life, you are everything to me. And also, I want you to know that I really do feel the love you have for me when you hold me in the twilight. When I'm feeling scared or lonely, you comforts and calms me, while reassuring my heart that all will be alright. Well, I'm just sending you this short message to let you know that I am still your bride and I'll be patiently waiting for your return. *Love, your Bride....*

Sing King

Sing king... Sing me a song. Sing me a heavenly song, a song that only you can sing. A song fit for the king's voice, flowing so musically from a voice of a king. It's a new song to his queen. So, sing my king... Sing to your lovely queen!

Here It Is

Her it is, here it is! Here is a fresh cut, fresh picked beautiful flower just for you!!! God loves you and I love you. Now love yourself and enjoy this beautiful day!

Receive It

Good days and bad days, we all have them. Yes, I know how you must feel. So, go ahead and praise our *Savior* now! And while you're praising him, thank Him for all the things He has and will do your life. Our *Heavenly Father* deserves our praise.... Repeat this *(x5):* I believe that God is turning some things *(state what it is that you want God to do for you)* around for me, right now in Jesus Name!!! Now, I hope and pray that through your faith, you believe and receive it, believing that it's already done in Jesus mighty and holy name, amen!

Someone Else

Let's take the time and pray for someone today. Pray for their salvation; don't worry about your situation. Why, because while you're praying for that someone else, God is interceding for you because you're interceding for someone else. Someone needs your prayers to make it! Now, before you continue to read any farther, stop and pray for 5 minutes "push" as they say, *pray until something happens*!!!

Let me help you..... Father in Jesus name, I pray for........................ *(State their name)* And I also pray for............................ *(State their name)* They need your help in *(finances, health, deliverance, marriage etc.)* Lord, please meet their needs in Jesus name, amen!

God

God- Brilliant, Wise, Sovereign, Omnipotent, Omnipresent, Good, Merciful, Kind, He's the I Am that I Am, the First and Last.

God- He's Genius and Smart, Faithful, He's Jehovah, and The Lover of my soul.

God- He's, All knowing, He's a Masterful Artist, Creator of All Things, All Powerful, and He's My Provider, He's Loving, and a Forgiver and the list goes on and on...

I just named a few, but who is God to you, can you name a few too? While you're telling Him who you know Him to be, make sure it's personal, I did!

Let's get started...God you are... *(My peace, my healer etc.)*

No Matter

Always remember, no matter what may come our way, all is well... No matter what may happen whether good or bad, God is still good, and God is still God! And no matter what trial I may face...I will think positive and I will speak positive! I will...I will!!!

Announcing

Announcing: Heavenly Praise Break...Heavenly Praise Break!!!

This is your time to give God, the best of your best praise. It's been held back for a long time. So give it all you've got.... Ready? 1, 2, 3, PRAISE HIM!!! Come on, you know that you have more in your reserve, let it be released!

Let's do it again, ready? 1, 2, 3, PRAISE HIM!!! Again...1, 2, 3, PRAISE HIM!!! Yes, that blockage had to be released.

I Hear

I hear sweet sounding music in the air; it's really a lovely song. I hear a song of victory oh my soul and it's approaching near, close to my ear, a song of praise and adoration. Therefore, fret not my dear child there's nothing to fear. It's a song of triumph, not in the natural just to be clear. But, I do hear a beautiful, beautiful song down in my spiritual ear; I hope this was made very clear about what I hear.

See About Me

I'm looking forward to our special appointment today. But don't worry; I'll be here waiting while longing to hear what you will say. I know you will come see about me, since you've always made time for us to sit and dine, which is always fine. So, please Lord, don't forget to come see about me during this time, between 12 and 9. Now if you wish at any other time, it will be fine. Just come see about me.

Enjoy

I'm sitting here thinking of you today. Let me ask you a question, how are you today? This moment is all about you *(Dear Reader)*. As I wrote this book I thought of you. *Reader*, be encouraged, remain faithful to the Lord, and remember that the joy of the Lord is your strength and may God shine his face on you today. Here's another question for you. How would you like a dozen of your favorite flowers to enjoy on this day? Now remember, these spiritual flowers are only for your eyes to see, enjoy them, be blessed and have a wonderful and glorious day!

Prophesy: God knows!

Can I prophesy to you for this season in your life? First, you must have faith and trust God for your spiritual overflow and trust God for what you do not know. Second, you must also believe and trust God for what you do not see. Why? Because only God knows what one day you will truly be, since the future God really does see.

God Love

A God kind of love is when you give your heart, mind, body, and soul to the Lord, feed the hungry, and clothe the naked. A God kind of love is when you give time when you don't have time to help someone spiritually in need. A God kind of love is when you choose to love someone who you know doesn't love you! A God kind of love is when you can deny yourself as Christ denied himself! Now that's love, God's love!

Speak It!

I am the lender, not the borrower! I am blessed! I am prosperous! You must speak it until you believe it... Now please repeat ....

Do It With Passion!

Whatever you do, do it with passion. If you exercise...Do it with passion! If you work...Do it with passion! When you sing...Do it with passion! When you worship...Do it with passion! If you clean...Do it with passion. If you cook...Do it with passion! When you serve...Do it with passion! I said all that to say this; if you say that you love God, then love God with everything you've got, and surely in doing that...This is Passion!

Here I Am

I was born to worship, here I am Lord, I come to worship! I was called to serve, so here I am Lord, and I am here to serve! I was told to go into the hedges and the highways, so here I am Lord send me, I'll go. Here I am Lord, Here I am!

Lift Me

Have you ever felt like you needed a little lift, or wished that you had a day at the spa? Well okay, relax and take some deep breaths and refresh yourself.

Say: Lord lift my heart...Lift my spirit...Lift my mind, where you are ...(x5) *(Please take deep breaths before saying it over and again.)*

Sing

If you never sung before, here is your time, repeat this:

I... Worship... You Lord...and I adore...You. (x5)

Wow!!! You really did sing! Now go ahead and make it personal, make it your own, as you sing to the Lord a new song. God hears you, keep on singing...sounds really good. *(Sing it again and let it flow directly from your heart.)*

❖ *There will never be room for Pride in real LOVE!*

Pep Talk

I think it's time to give you another pep talk today *(smile)*,
says the Lord. "HOLD YOUR HEAD UP ANYWAY... NO
MATTER WHAT COMES YOUR WAY!" Enough said, Says
the Lord, together we got this! YES, WE GOT THIS! Now,
be on your way until our next pep talk on another day.

A Light?

Need a light or do you have a light? The light in the night, are you
talking the stars and the moon? Not quite, its God our *Fathers*
(son) *Jesus Christ* the light of the world, shining at it's brightest
even in the darkest of night. But no need to fear you can still use
your spiritual and natural nightlight. But to set the record straight,
the sun (*Son*) will always be the brightest of all lights, so let your
light forever shine and glorify your *Father* which is in heaven. We,
the children of God should always keep our light on, to help light
the path for those still in darkness. Now, do you have the light?

Winner

A good fighter is when they get knocked down and rises back up again
even stronger and wins the fight. Now, that's powerful! *(Conquer)*

❖ *When you pray…pray hard!*

Let Go

Do not be afraid! Ever been scared to let go of the blanket or something that you may have had for a very long time? What about those old clothes and shoes pushed in the back of your closet, knowing that you will never wear them again?

Okay, pause, take moment and think of everyone who has offended you and caused the pain that you often feel...is it painful, I thought so.

Now take a deep, deep, deep breath and say, Lord, I let them/it go and I forgive them for the pain that I feel. I realize that it wasn't the person. So, I pray against the spiritual forces that have come up against me to break me and tear me down to make my life miserable. Today I choose to let it go, and I will walk and live a life of spiritual abundance, in my health, finances etc. In Jesus mighty name I pray, amen!

Sooooo...Good

God is good! God is good! God is sooooo good!!! I beat you to the punch, didn't I? Now, you say it, God is good! God is good! God is sooooo good!!! And just for your knowledge there is not a type-o in this. Isn't God good!

Me Again

Hi, Jesus it's me again. I was here thinking about you again. *(Smile)* Recently, I have found myself thinking of you over and over again. I think of how you've watched over me, when I had no idea that you were there. Oh, how about when you blessed me, when I thought I was forgotten, thank you? Let me not mention how you healed me, thank you! Oh yea, and I have a sound mind, I can think for myself, thank you! *(Smile)* I wish I knew a word that means more than "Thank you" Well, Lord from my heart to yours, I'll say what I know, "THANK YOU!"

Another

I feel another praise coming on, as the song says, and I gotta let it out. Why don't you sing it! You will feel so much better. Clap your hands too! If you don't know the song, say this, I feel a praise...Coming on! (x10) Hallelujah!

Redeemer!!!

God: Sovereign, Compassionate, Kind, Loving, Trustworthy, Gentle, Merciful, Ultimate and only Forgiver of man's sins! There's *No other* God, like our God*! Redeemer*

Refreshing

Refreshing as a cool spring breeze is God to the soul! *Refresh...*

Twist

Twist, the bible says that a threefold cord is not easily broken. Why? Well every strand is tied together tightly or joined together. There is a (twist), something hidden in this message, read it until you get it! Hint: Make sure the Lord is in it...It's not hard!

All It Took

Lemonade, lemon cake, lemon jello, lemon cookies, and we can't forget about the ole time favorite, lemon meringue pie. Wow, something so good can come from that sour and bitter fruit. All it took was a twist!

Looked Pass

God is... Love, wow! Yes, God is love and His love is forever and ever. (*Teardrop*) Gods love is merciful, He looked pass all my sins! Who wouldn't, tell me who wouldn't serve a God like this!

Life Has Choices

Life has choices; therefore we must pray that we make the right one today. For we know tomorrow is not promised.

So, *Father* in Jesus name! Thank you for leading me and directing me. Thank you for helping me to make wise choices. Thank you for forgiving me and encouraging me, even when I have made wrong choices. *Father* I acknowledge you as part of my life, head of my life, and being my life, as I breathe your breath daily through my lungs. I know, without you in my life I can do nothing.

So, I trust, *Holy Father* that you will continue to help me make the right choices daily, and then I will glorify you as I walk in your wisdom in this world among those without. As I remember that life has choices, I will also remember that every choice I make have consequences. (*Wisdom*)

Not Wrong

Loving God our *Savior* is not wrong! However, loving the world more than we love God our *Savior* is! That's just plain wrong!!! Which one will you love more, the right one or the wrong one? Think about it.

Saturate

Saturate my soul my Lord, pour into me and flood
my thirsty and over dried soul. Oh how I love thee, oh
Lord. Oh how I really, really love thee. *(Saturate)*

Shower Down

Shower down your sweet grace. Grace and strength to do what I
need to do. That inner grace that only you can give and you only
can see. Come on dear Lord and shower down, shower me over and
over as you please. Yes, dear Lord this is a great need, so come on
and shower down, shower down, shower down on little ole me.

In My Heart (Repeat x1)

I love thee Lord Jesus. I will forever love thee! In my heart for
eternity, I love thee! Forever and ever till all eternity....

❖ *What a day, what a day, what another opportunity*
to be able to praise our Loving Savior!!!

The Best!

Great job and well done!!! You're a wonderful artist; we see your work in full display every single day because you are the one who painted the heavens. You're a self made millionaire, who owns the most cattle on thousands of hills. Oh and what was that, you are Lord of all creation, and K*ing of Kings*?

Wow, I must stop now and say "what a *Mighty God* we serve!" Oh, and you created the heavens and the earth, wow! God you are truly amazing! You're the best *Father* of *all*; yes, you are truly awesome, the greatest, superb, stupendous, marvelous, well, simply put you're the best. I had to boast a little about my Father! Truly our *Heavenly Father* is the BEST!

Today

Today Lord, I know that you have spoken a blessing over my life. Why? I feel it in my bones. *Smile*

The prophet Jeremiah said it best when he said, "It feels like fire shut up in my bones."

So, Lord, I feel it... I feel it!

Today, I feel blessings all in my bones!!! *Smile*

Yes, all in my bones....

➢ *Another Reflection*

Dear Jesus, here I am again. I have come to worship.
Worship is what I do. To worship you sweet Jesus is
what I was born and created to do. *Surrender*

Oh my sweet Jesus, you are very dear to me. And Jesus, please
continue to speak softly in my ear. Oh my sweet, sweet, and precious
Jesus, when you talk it comes loud and clear so don't worry, I will
hear, knowing that your approach is so near. *Remembrance*

Heavens music is playing me a lovely song. Harps, violins,
flute and Chellos are quieting my weary and tired little soul.
Play on song; play me a lovely heavenly song. *Hear*

As the white snow falls and blankets the entire earth, so
does our *Heavenly Fathers* love covers all of us. *Comfort*

Pure are you oh Lord, pure are you. No blemish, no
blemish to see, in you it will not be. *Holy*

Tenderly speaking to my heart is our *Father's* voice. *Teardrop*

➤ *__Another Reflection__*

Cry to our *Savior*, let our voices be heard and
tell Him all of our problems. *Heart*

Surrounding me with your tender touch...thinking of how I will
forever love you, love you, love you, very much! *Eternal*

Holding me close is like you Lord, holding me to
your heart never letting me go. *Forever*

Step by step my dear Lord, shall you guide me step by step. *Dependence*

A drip here and a drip there, isn't it good to have to a drip
of God's goodness flowing all in the air? *Saturate*

Like a leaf blowing in the wind are we without God in our lives. *Choice*

Thank you Jesus, I really do feel your prayers covering
me, because every time something hinders me, you
always come to set me free. *Faithfulness*

❖ *This is a day for me to feast on Gods true character.*

➢ *Another Reflection*

There is a highway, but we must choose the
right one to travel on. *Wisdom*

Running and tired, tired of running. But we must
keep running into our *Fathers* arms. *Reward*

Forever praise will be on my lips. Then my soul will rejoice and
my heart will begin to sing a new heavenly song. *Thankful*

Loving our *Creator* is all I want to do.... *Love*

My mind will forever think of the many wonders that
our *Almighty God* has done! *Appreciation*

Day by day, you will lead me forever and a day. *Acknowledge*

The awesomeness of your power has and will always
be shown to all of eternity. *Gratitude*

➢ *__Another Reflection__*

Forever and always are Gods gracefulness and compassion, His mercy and forgiveness is extended to all of his beautiful creation. *Heart*

Yes dear Lord, I will not cease to forever pray. *Selah*

Accept my praise and accept my true worship. *Devotion*

Loving God more than loving this world is priceless. *Wisdom*

Thank you Lord for continuing to heal my very deep wounds, I will forever be grateful. *Appreciation*

Here waiting for my *Heavenly Father* to do more work in my life. *Anticipating*

Some people are fully grown, but yet still a child in heart. *Humility*

➤ *Another Reflection*

God is always reachable and never too far
that He cannot be touched. *Selah*

Tranquility, tranquility, there's nothing like good old tranquility. *Peace*

Having a special moment with the one I love
leaves my soul speechless. *Eternal*

Fill me up Lord, I've been emptied but now ready to receive.
I'm ready to receive more of your Godly character and
some extra doses of your spiritual goodness. *Saturate*

Saturate my hungry and thirsty soul with little drips
of your love and I'll be satisfied. *Comfort*

When I go through the storm, God you will protect me. *Security*

Forever God is to say, forever priceless. *Teardrop*

➤ *Another Reflection*

Fresh anointing, come and let your *Holy Spirit* flow. Let it fall on me as the dew that falls from heaven in the early morning. *Showers*

The spiritual bride and groom will always be one. *Forever Love*

Holy Spirit, I am forever captured by your love,
loving me ever so tenderly. *Heart*

Say what David said; create in me a clean heart
oh God. And refresh... *(Psalms 51) KJV*

Worship God oh my soul, worship God! *Cleanse*

I'm yours Lord, always and forever. *Belonging*

I welcome you *Holy Spirit* into my heart, so you can continue to do more of your wonderful art, and make me a clean heart. *Surrender*

A Reason

When God placed time and seasons, it was a reason. Yes, a reason to press, no matter the season. Time is given in every second and minute of the day, whether it's hot or cold, busy or slow. Let's not forget there's always a reason, knowing God set time in every given season.

Love Is

In the dictionary, love is a word, but love is real. Love is alive, oh yes, love talks and love walks. Love shows and tells, love heals and love forgives. Love is forever, my dear friend that's what love is.

True Praise

True praise is what I really want say's the Lord, a genuine and an unselfish praise. Let it be real and let it come from your heart, and then a true praise is what I will surely get. *(Teardrop)*

❖ *This is a day for me to feast on Gods true character...*

I Believe

Yes Lord, I do believe! I believe you healed the lepers
stated in the bible, and I believe that you healed the
blind man's eyes. Yes Lord, I do believe! *(Faith)*

Love Shows!

Like a mountain covered in soft white snow, love shows! Love, like trees
are colored in green and the sky is painted in blue, love shows! Love
is in the warm and cool crisp wind, blowing daily across my delicate
and smooth skin. I said it before, and I say it again "Love Shows!"

Self Encourage

Encouragement is what we all need. So I'll encourage myself:

Self! Be Encouraged! Self I say, "Be Encouraged!!!"

Self gets a little stubborn and rebellious sometime and doesn't
always want to listen or submit, so I need to say it again...

"SELF...You will be ENCOURAGED!!!" *You'll make it through this day!*

Praise Break

Praise Break! Praise Break! Hallelujah!!! (x3)

It's time for another praise break...praise is in the air. *Praise Him*
with your lips. *Praise your God* and *Savior!*!! Come on and clap those
hands, stump those feet, even if they are a size 11 or 12. *(Smile)*
Praise is what we do! It really does feel good to praise the Lord!

Tickle, Tickle

Listen, I know that most of us do not like to take medicine.
But here is some meds for you today, tickle, tickle, and now
laugh!!! Let's try that again, tickle, tickle, tickle, and laugh!!!
I knew it was down in there! Next time don't wait so long
and please take your meds daily. Tickle, Tickle, Tickle!!!

Have a happy and healthy day!

Little, Big

Little things can mean so much. Appreciate God for
the little then one day, the *Bigger* will come.

Bird's Eye

Can you picture yourself, as if you're looking down at a bird's eye view?
Wow, the world is so big! Let's get out the box, the sky is the limit!

Dear Friend

My dear friend, how are you? I'm looking to see you soon.
I've been thinking of you, remembering those times we were
together. Yes, you had me laughing when I should have been
crying. I know, I know, you'll be back later this week or maybe
sooner. Well, this letter is already in the mail. Love you, friend!

❖ *Forever, Jewels of…Knowledge, wisdom, and understanding*

Feel

Lord, the way you make me feel, you makes me love myself. The way you make me feel, you makes me encourage myself. And the way that you make me feel, I love you more and more.

Stop & Breathe

Stop and breathe, take some deep breaths and say:
Thank you Jesus! Thank you Jesus! *(x5)*

(Take a couple of minutes to relax and refresh!)

Make It Sweet!

There is a spiritual tree way up in the heavens. But a strange thing has happened, good delicious fruit is falling and no one is catching the lemons. Hey, if you get the lemons, you can make the bitter-sweet! Think about it! *(Life)*

Chosen

When God chose David, "A Man after Gods Own Heart" He chose the best! When God chose Jonah, He chose the best! When God chose Mary-the mother of Jesus, He chose the best! When God chose *Jesus* "His only begotten son", He chose the best! And when God chose you and me, He still... chose the best! Now be glad about it....

Eat

Question, did you eat your daily bread today?
Well, if you didn't, please don't forget.

Read: *Matthew: 4th chapter*

Okay, I know you are enjoying "Forever, Jewels" But, first read the Word
of God, then come back and finish reading Forever, Jewels. *(Smile)*

Different Ways

As there are many different species of butterflies, there are many
different ways to worship. Worship is our own personal way to
express our self's, while speaking to God through our inner spirit
and outer body. So, now is your time to worship God with your
mind, soul and body.... Let's begin... "Lord, I worship you" etc.

Search My Heart

Lord God...

Tell me what do you see in me? Look way down, deep! Deep as
your eyes can go and search my heart and my spirit...Cleanse
me and I shall be clean, for your eyes are as fire, red and shining,
purer than pure. Yes my lord, your eyes are surely the finest.

The Dew Will Do

Lord God...If you don't rain on me, I'll settle for the dew, the
morning dew, like the fresh anointing from Aaron's beard or maybe
the crumbs from the rich man's table. Yes, Lord that will do!

Another Day

Lord, it's another day's journey and I'm so glad. Lord if it's
not a bother, please prepare me for the journey ahead.
And this little sentence has been well said. *Amen.*

Where

Reflecting on Gods goodness, where did the time go? And
thinking of Gods splendor, where did the time go? I have served
and I'm still serving. Oh lord, where did the time go?

Forever Mine

Forever you are mine before the world ever begun, until
the very end of time! Forever we belong, forever, and
ever you will always be mine! Yours forever....

In The Wind

Listen, it has begun, listen closely, and attentively, my dear friend;
his voice is in the wind. It may be quiet or sometimes even silent;
listen my friend, because Gods voice is quietly speaking in the wind!

Everyday Love

What is an everyday love? An everyday love is to forgive.
Forgive? Yes, every day we must forgive, that's an everyday
love. God loves you, and did I mention that He forgave
you to? Well, He do, so have anyone offended you?

Morning/Night Song

A song in the morning, a song in the night. Come sing to me my lover,
sing to me my knight. A song in the morning mixed with a song in
the night? Oh, yes how wonderful it is to dance in the moonlight!

Not Alone

Thank you Jesus! I am not alone!

(Please repeat until Gods *Holy Spirit* rest upon you!)

Repeat (x10)

The Lord, Is

The Lord is my *"All That!"* I shall not want. So, I am healthy, wealthy
and rich! The lord is my *"All That!"* so I am whole and I am healed.
The lord is my *"All That!"* Therefore, I have plenty, and I have more
than enough! The Lord is my shepherd, I shall not want! *Shalom!*

Loud or Whisper

Whether we grew up poor or wealthy, or we have little or much,
let us not forget how far we have come. Whether we hear
it loud or hear it in a quiet whisper, "ALL WE HAVE" comes
from the lord, who has made the heavens and earth.

Stand In Awe

Stand in awe my soul, stand in awe! My soul loves Jesus and I
thank God, Jesus loves me! Stand in awe my soul, stand in awe!

Rest

Rest my soul, in the lord! Rest, I say in the Lord! Rest....

My Sacrifice

Here's my sacrifice, my heart and my mind I willfully give to thee. It's been slightly bruised, little bit damaged and may even be a little broken too...but it's me, my only sacrifice. I hear that you can fix it for free, so I give you all of me. *(Teardrop)*

Our Eye

Holy Spirit, as the sun illuminates threw the ever changing sky, let your sun shine through our natural-spiritual eyes (red, yellow, blue, green, black, brown or gray)...Let the sunshine of your holiness brightly illuminate into our eye.

Hi!

Hi Jesus, it's me again. I don't want anything I just wanted to say, hi! I'll talk with you later, God's willing.

Be Different

Dare to be different! Dare to be new! Dare to be different and change your view. Let God make you completely and totally new. Now...That's something to chew! Can you digest that?

Cooling Waters

Tap into the cool waters, the deep springs are running. The springs are running slowly, giving us time to smell the nearby roses. Springs are flowing, colors of blue with the smell of the mornings new. Tap into the heavenly, a spiritual refreshing of our *Fathers* crisp cooling waters.

Peace/Quiet

Peace and quiet, no birds are chirping. Peace and quiet, there's stillness in the air. Peace and quiet, peace and quiet... Awe....

Nations Crying

Do you hear the people, nations crying? Yes my Lord, yes. But what are they saying? We need a word ... We need a word! Lord please help us, we desperately need a word!

Cup of Tea

I have a special visit today, we're having tea and the tea is mixed just right, not too sweet. This visit is not only for me, but it's for us three. Now enjoy your spiritual cup of tea with Jesus, you, and me.

My Time

What am I doing with my time? What's on my mind? Am I wisely using my time or should I whine? Time is valued just as precious as a dime. Spend it wisely!

As One

Together, let us worship the *Father*, and worship the *son*.
Let us worship them as one. Together...Let us praise Him
to the lowest valley, praise Him to the highest mountain.
Let us praise the *Father* and the Son together as one.

Right Now

My soul wishes to bless you in the morning. My soul wishes to bless
you in the evening. My soul wishes to bless you in the night watches. I
will bless the lord right now, my soul! I will bless the lord, right now!!!

Bucket

God is releasing spiritual jewels today, and the jewels are
falling. Falling down from the heavens, are Jewels of wisdom,
love, kindness, patience, etc. I have put some in my bucket,
now don't forget yours. Some people may think you're lucky,
But when God fills your bucket he calls you blessed.

Have a blessed day!

Appreciate

Lord, I appreciate my guardian angel. Your holy angel's that
you assign to me daily. They watches over me, protects me
from all harm, and they encourages me to move forward in life.
But most of all, I appreciate you my Lord, I appreciate you!

No Strings

Loving you lord is what I do. No strings attached!

Loving you Lord is a must. I do not have to act.

Loving you lord, with no strings attached!

Love Me

Love me now, love me forever.

When first I wake up, love me.

Before I wash my face, love me forever.

Before I brush my teeth or shower, love me.

If I don't wear the finest of perfume or apparel, love me.
Whenever I seem quiet or silent, love me forever.

Love me forever, Lord Jesus, love me forever....

❖ *Love yourself, love God first then love the rest.*

Best

Thank you for loving me when I've said things I didn't really mean. However, to be clean in my heart is what I mean. Lord you know living in this life is only a test, only show me how to love myself. Since loving is what you do best.

Blurred Vision

Forgive when I'm having a bad day especially when I have too much to say. Forgive me Lord, when I go astray walking in the wrong way. And please Lord; forgive me when I have made the wrong decision because it blurs my clear vision.

Stood the Light

Let there be light and the light shined and shined...And darkness came and darkness left and the light shined... And kept on shining.... And the darkness came again and left. Then, the light shined and shined, and shined...Till there was no more darkness and there stood only the light! And it shined and shined and shined and shined.

Check

Before being first in the line at the department store, first in line at the grocery store, first to get that long awaited pay check, or maybe you are met with the waiter bringing that delicious food check. We know we must all give to the IRS! So, keep God first because it only keeps our heart in check.

Neither

Do you complain about the little bit of money you have or do you boast about all the money you have? Ask yourself this: which one is better, complaining or boasting? *(God's answer: neither)*

Breather

Taking a breather is like a breath of fresh air, clean air that quiets the soul...letting your peace create in and around me tranquility...Like the sound of calm running waters and jumping in a spa refreshing my weary soul....

Tears of Joy, Let It Flow

Something is happening, I cannot explain. I feel your *Holy Spirit*, Lord let it flow.... *(Teardrop)*

Weekdays

Monday, Tuesday, Wednesday, Thursday, Friday, Saturday and sometimes Sunday, is a busy week for many of us... Let us not forget to rest and give God one day. Then we will surely find rest for our weary soul...

Ever Heard

Have you ever heard this: never give up, never quit? Well... God has invested so much in all of us...He formed us; shaped us and then He made us all in his wonderful image! God started us and He wants to finish. Therefore, we should never give up and never quit...Then God can see His finished product-*You*!

Free Vacation

Want a free vacation? No gimmicks...Find a quiet place in the house, around the house, to the park, or maybe at the beach. Get away it doesn't cost anything... Enjoy yourself! Truly, this could be a mini enjoyable vacation and it's all free. *(Smile)*

WOW!

Wow...what a long day! What a God given day....LOL! I won't complain! Yes, I say...What a day, what a day!

Now breathe...

And relax....

Ever Said

Have you ever said it was January and now it's August? How time flies. Well, at least we are here to say it...*LOL!*

No Room

Think of all the good things that have happened in your life. Now think of all the good things that you forget about daily. Pause... Now there's no room left to complain. Thank you Lord!

❖ *Lord, only you are worthy of all honor and praise, you stand alone in the fullness of your glory and splendor.*

Feel Like

My soul is saying... I feel like blessing the Lord right now, I
feel like saying... Thank you Jesus! I really just want to praise
him!!! My heart is rejoicing and my heart is singing! Awe...
Now my soul is at ease and my soul is pleased....

Drizzle/Flood

Receiving a little is sometimes better than receiving a lot.
A drizzle can be better than a flood. So, let us learn how to
receive and be thankful for both the little and the lot. My
prayer is, Lord help me to be content in Jesus name, Amen!

Refreshing Moments

Sitting and thinking of refreshing moments in the mind, while
whispering moments of peace...yes, silence in the air. Tranquility within
a Hawaiian breeze, waiting to be ceased when there is whispering
moments of nighttime zzzzzzz's. And when I awake, then I can
say "Thank you Jesus" now I'm feeling renewed and refreshed.

Let It Flow

Letting the Word of God flow through our veins is like having
a day at the spa feeling clean and refreshed with warm
bubbles blowing... Jacuzzi here I come... Waiting just for
you, now is your time...refresh yourself in the word daily, it
will be like having a free spa with no strings attached.

God Is

Love is light, love is God. God is love, love is eternal. Love is pure, love is real. Love is God, God is good! Love is forever, God is Omega. Love is the beginning and love has no end! God is.... *(Heavenly)*

Capture

A sweet smelling fragrance is something that captures our attention. We must be just that, and then we can capture God's attention!

I Come

Lord, I come to you as I am, I have not much to say; but I come just as I am. Yes, I am only clay, but I come as I am. Remember Lord, I have not much to say...

Waiting

Waiting for my special moment, and waiting for my special day. Stay with the Lord I say, "Soul...Stay with the Lord!" And you will see that glorious day!

Just Thinking

Lord, in my mind, I'm thinking about what you've done for me and thinking of how you have set me free. Also, I'm thinking of your love and thinking of your grace. Oh my Lord, how I long to see your majestic face! Yes... I was just sitting here thinking....I hope you're okay with that....

Joined

My Love, I belong to you, only you, and just for you!
Forever, I am yours! Forever you are mine! We are
joined together forever and ever and ever...

Beautiful Song

I hear beautiful songs upon my bed, as I lay my tired and little heavy
head. I'm hearing a voice like no other, songs from my dearly beloved.
I know that His approach is near, because He's singing me sweet,
sweet, melodies that only I hear. It's songs of comfort inside my
spiritual ear. Oh, yes! Sing me another beautiful song my love, sing.

Faithfully Waiting

(Bride) I am faithfully waiting for you my love, patiently anticipating
your return. (Groom) There's no need to worry, my dear...Because,
forever you are my only love; so, please do not shed a single tear.

Faithfully yours...

Psalms 9:2

I will be glad and rejoice in thee: I will sing praise
to thy name, o thou most high. (KJV)

Now begin to repeat and worship:

The Lord God is my strength and song, you are my eternal hope and
your train fills my heart. I will be glad and rejoice in thee: I will sing
praise to your name, oh Lord, the strength and redeemer of my soul.

Tickle

Oh No! Did you take you medicine today? Don't worry, open wide... Tickle, come on...Tickle, tickle. Almost, a little bit more... Tickle, tickle, tickle. (LOL) Go ahead and admit it, you know you feel better now.... Love you!

Psalms 21:13

Be thou exalted, Lord, in thine own strength: so will we sing and praise thy power. (KJV)

Here am I oh Lord, I present to you my mind and mine own will, to submit and surrender, I am not mine but yours. So, I come to worship... I come to exalt you and only you! I dance for you and you only; around your throne I dance, because you are worthy. How beautiful are you my groom, my husband...*How beautiful*!

Psalms 22:22

I will declare thy name unto my brethren: in the midst of the congregation will I praise thee. (KJV)

To declare and make known my Lord, I will not be ashamed. I will speak of who you are and I will not hold my peace. I will also declare thy name and I will not forget to praise thee. I will not forget!

Shine!

Shine on, *King Jesus*! Shine on! Let the earth, produce, let
it display your glory from above. Let the heavens show
your face. And may you rest through the moon.

Shine on *King Jesus*!!! Go ahead and shine on,
the glory belongs to you alone. *Shine!!!*

Psalms 23:1

The Lord is my shepherd; I shall not want. (KJV)

I thank you Lord, for being my teacher, and my master.
Thank you for watching over me with your loving care.
Thanks for being my supplier, and my life giver,
because of who you are I will never lack!
I am the head and never the tail!
I am above only and never beneath!
I am truly a shepherd's child! I know who I am, and who's I am!
I am a child of a Shepherd King and my *Father* is rich....

"You own every cattle, the earth is yours *Heavenly Father.* The silver
and gold is yours and I am a rightful heir to everything you own."
Thank you *Father* or should I just call you daddy
for all you have done. *(Xoxoxo)*

Beautiful Too!

I love myself, because God made me. I Love myself,
because God makes everything good. I am beautiful
and God is good. God made me this way.
When God made me in his image, God allowed me to
reflect his character in my heart, soul, and spirit.
So truly, God is beautiful and His beauty lives inside.
And that makes me beautiful too!
Amen and amen!

Rest... (Repeat x2)

Rest in the Lord....My soul!

I say rest in the Lord.
Rest, I say, In the Lord!
Be encouraged my soul!
Be encouraged!

I will... (Repeat x4)

I will worship the Lord in my mind.
I will worship the Lord my soul.
I will worship the Lord!!!
For I will press.... My soul, I will press...

Quiet Whispers

Yes, Lord I do hear you calling me, it's not loud, but I hear you.
I am not afraid, because it's you. Talk to me more my love, I'm
here and I'm listening. I hear your voice and only you will I follow.
Keep talking my Lord, keep talking...in quiet whispers, in quiet
whispers my Lord please... keep speaking to my heart.

Daily

Choosing to have God in our life daily is like having a fresh
cool shower, on a hot scorching day. And as the water
cleanses the dirtiness away, God cleanses our soul daily
and our sins are completely washed and carried away.

Smile

People would often say, "Have a drink it's on me."
Well, I say have a "BIG SMILE"
It's on me. Now, I hope and pray this has made your day. *LOL!!!*

It's Coming

I feel another one coming; I feel it coming... It's
BIG! Here it is, it's a...It's a smile!!!
Have a blessed day... Love you!

You Say!

So you say, you had a rough day, Oh no!
Well, okay your not sure...that's better!
Remember, Remember, let's appreciate
because, someone is always worse!

Desperation!

Desperately running and running, heavily breathing and sweating
while never having a mind to give up. I'm persistent! I see Him (Jesus)
my eternal goal and finish line of my faith. He is the reason why I'm
still in this race. Bruised, but still running, running with an eternal
purpose. Jesus, the Lover of my soul! My reason, my purpose!

Deep Hole

Have some one ever hurt you? Well, if you think hard enough you
probably have hurt someone too? So, forgive! Remember, we all reap
what we have sown. If you forgive, then you will be set free. Yes, I
know what was done, feels as though a deep whole was punched
right in your heart! But please forgive and then the hole inside
that you feel will disappear and then God will began to make you
whole again. And best of all, our *Heavenly Father* will forgive you.

Now doesn't that feel good to know?
(Forgive & Smile again))

❖ *Let go of all the pain and hurt, it's too much for us to carry say's, the Lord!*

Psalms 30:5

<u>Weeping</u> or is it laughter? Is it a wedding or is it a
new job, you've been praying for? *(Teardrop)*

<u>Endure</u>; yes, endure the hard times that seems as though
you are all alone and hopeless, but, knowing deep in
your heart that God is still with you. *(Heart)*

<u>Night</u>, how long is a night? Having nights, that feels as long
as years. But, still able to see the breaking of day! *(Hope)*

<u>Joy</u> oh wow!!! Finally my strength is renewed and my joy is restored
and fulfilled! Thank you Lord, you never left me alone. *(Strength)*

<u>Morning</u>, after all the weeping during hard times, and experiencing
sleepless nights, joy has come! Yes, now I'm a little bit stronger
and living a life with my Jesus every day. Hello Sunday morning
and hello...*Son*-shine it's a new and brighter day. *(Smile!)*

Hello, How Are You Today?

I don't know what time of day it will be when you read this.
But, if you are or will be serving God faithfully, I want you to
know that your latter will be greater! I Please, believe it!

Now receive it!

Love Is God

Love is powerful; love is deep, deeper than the deep blue sea...
Love is wide, wider than the universe. Love smells good, just
as the Rose of Sharon and Lilly of the Valley... Love taste like
sweet honey, hidden way down in the honeycomb... Love falls
sometimes fast and slow, like fresh cooling rain, the former
and latter rain together... Love is beautiful, love is God.

Time

God wants you to love Him more; if you take the time to talk to Him,
He will discuss more in depth with you. So go ahead, I'll help you get
started... *Dear Heavenly Father*.....please show me how to love you
more as I sacrifice more by, praying more and..........................(Fill In)
I'm so proud of you, now go on and tell Him more, yes...He's still listening.

Jewel

Have you had a jewel lately? This valuable jewel is called hope;
in Jesus name... Receive it, since you know you need it!!

Hello.....Again

- ❖ God says, that you are beautiful...you are one of a kind.
- ❖ God says... He loves you!
- ❖ God wants you to know that He will never leave nor forsake you!
- ❖ STOP! Slow down! Read *(Mark 6:31)* God wants you to take it easy...too!

Excited

Oh, I'm so excited, so excited! Now I will open my eyes and see the new present. O my...Thank you, thank you, Lord it's a new day! Now, I will truly cherish and enjoy it! *(Thankful)*

How Do You Feel?

Let me ask you a question. When is the last time you opened up and confessed your sins? If it's been a while, please look to heaven and start now, it's ok. You'll feel so much better and happier that you did. *(Forgiveness)*

Psalms 23 (Fill In)

The Lord is my *Shepherd.*
The Lord is my _____ (Fill In)
The Lord is my *Healer.* The Lord is my keeper.
He is my *Strong Tower* and my *Defender.*
The Lord is my *Comforter* and my_____ (Fill In)
The Lord is *Everything,* I need Him to be.
Shalom!

Allow vs. Disallow

Question, what will you allow to trouble you today?
Here is a word of wisdom for you... Don't let
anything...I mean anything; mess up a
"Lovely Day" that the good Lord has given you. Please, don't allow negative thoughts, bad dreams or negative people give you a negative outcome. What you disallow, you resist! If it's lovely, just, pure, holy, or of good report then receive! *(Eternal)*

❖ *Remember (Jesus) our mediator is praying for you today!*

You Are

Holy are you oh Lord.
You are holy within and holy without.
Yes holy, holy, holy you are.
Righteous are you Lord, who having no wrong to comprehend.
Merciful, so merciful... Your mercy and compassion
only makes me more grateful.
So, I will say "I love you, I love you!" if I may.
Since, there are no other words to say.
(Heart Expressions)

Lately?

Have you received a jewel lately?
Here is a big bowl of ...LOVE! LOVE! LOVE! Now,
make sure it falls...completely all over you.
Again and again! *(Smile)*

Repeat/Refresh

I take this moment to refresh and say, I love you!
I love you Lord, I love you!
Now close your eyes Repeat (x10) *(Tranquility)*

Through It All

Despite what I have been through,
God loves me...Despite challenges that will come,
God is for me... Despite times I may fall short,
God holds me up... Despite the test and trials
that will come, God, I'll still serve you!
I know in my heart through it all...
God, you still love me *(Endurance)*

So Dear

Speaking in my ear ever so softly,
Just as morning dew.
I'm being very attentive to your voice
Lord, so please, let me hear.
Receiving direction in my spirit, since, you're so near.
I'm making preparations from what I hear, while holding
your words in my heart so dear. *(Embrace)*

Tell Me

Tell me, which will you have a good and blessed
day? Or, will you have a bad horrific day?
Which will you choose? *(Choice)*

Royal Seed (Repeat x3)

I must speak it!!!
I am blessed, I am loved! I am yours.
I am your child, a king's child!
I am part of a royal seed.
Yes, that's who I am!
I am a blessed seed of the king! *(Knowing)*
(Let it get down in your spirit)!

What Love?

What love do I feel; it is my *Father's* love?
He loves me when I need it most.
What kind of love is this?
This is unconditional and extreme agape love.
Where did this kind of love come from?
This kind of love only comes from our *Heavenly Father*
above; He wants us to experience all that He has for us.
Question, do you feel the warmth and comfort
of His sweet love, warming your heart?
Yes, this feeling is real... Just open your heart
and let love do its work *(Acceptance)*

Bright

Shining ever so brightly, your light illuminates my path.
Your son (Jesus) lights my path in every way.
Your holy angels surrounding me daily waiting patiently for their
masters say. Now I know my life is bright because it's filled with your
magnificent and glorious light. Lord, I remember what you said in
St. John, 14:6 "You are the Way, Truth, and the Life. (KJV)
I'm happy, because as long as I stay with you, then I'm
sure that my path will be light, right and bright!
Amen! *(Love)*

Lifted

Your love has lifted me in the way that I feel and the way I think.
Lord, your agape love has lifted my spirit and made me fresh and
renewed. Hallelujah for your eternal love! Lord, your love has
elevated me, like a hot air balloon... but only it's cool. *(Smile)*

Have You?

Have you laughed today? Okay... Here it is...are you ready?
Come on, pull it out... Tickle, tickle, tickle, almost there tickle,
tickle, tickle, now laugh! You did really good.... *(Smile)*

Light Enough

There is a sweet melody playing, and it sounds like a heavenly flute,
an organ, and a violin; it's a beautiful, beautiful sound that's playing
in the air. Listen precious child, sometimes burdens gets extremely
heavy. So, while you're meditating and listening to the melodies,
let God make your burdens light enough for you to carry. *(Peace)*

Pour

Rain, rain, please, don't go away!
However, since you're standing at my door let me say "I need more!"
Here's my cup Lord... I'm thirsty, need I say more. So, pour, pour,
and pour, while opening for you is my spiritual door. *(Heart)*

Date

Here meditating, and feeling so much better. Yes, I just ate
everything you have put on my plate. This special moment
was like eating a delicious meal while on a memorable date.
And for desert you fed me my favorite lemon cake. Thank you
Lord, for this wonderful and special date! *(Appreciation)*

Encouragement

Uh oh, are you ready for this? Open up and receive this big, humungous bowl of... Encouragement!!! Please, don't thank me, God knew you needed it. Be ENCOURAGED!

Special Prayer

Today, Lord I would like to pray for all who have ever did me wrong. Please bless them, change their heart and let them live a life that's pleasing in your sight. Now Lord, please help me to forgive them, then I will be totally free. *(Teardrop)*

Search

Search me Lord, search my heart.
Search me; I know you're near, not far. Search me
Oh God, as I shed a tear drop. I dare to say to you, my Lord, "chop, chop." But Lord you hear my "longing to be near you heart."
(Passion)

A Pair

Whispering nuggets of wisdom, knowledge and understanding, one cannot see them in a stare. Delicious nuggets are yours to take without having a dare. Please have some, for God does give threes in a pair.

You and Me

If only in my mind... Lord you belong only to me.
You are all mine and I am yours. What joy to know
that no one will come between us.
Forever you will be for me and
I will be for you. And when I awake there's only
you and me. *(One) and (Forever)*

All Is

I must tell myself, that all is well. I must say
It again, "ALL IS WELL!"
Now, I will take a deep breath and say,
"ALL IS WELL" with my soul. Now rest. *(Refreshed)*

Refresh

Give me more of you. I want all of your goodness.
Refresh my spirit anew. Yes, that's right my Lord,
I'm no good without you. So here am I, ready in mind and
open in heart. Waiting for you to make me new...

Silent Praise

Have you ever done a silent praise before? Let's do one now. Think
of all the good things that the *Almighty God* has done in your life
and begin to give Him an inward, quiet praise. Now, close your eyes
and begin, make sure you thank Him at the end. *(Thankfulness)*

Need

Holy Spirit, I adore you. I really need you in my life. You bring me joy,
you give me peace. You show me love and comfort me. *Holy Spirit*,
I'm so glad that you chose to dwell in someone like
me. You are truly my need! *(Heartbeat)*

Hallelujah!!!

To the *Most High God*, Hallelujah He reigns, He reigns!!! Hallelujah
to the God and the *Creator* of the universe! Lord God, you reign,
you reign! Hallelujah, hallelujah, hallelujah!!! *(Adoration)*

Only For You

I will forever adore you, my light and my salvation. *My Savior*, you are
the hope and joy of my existing life. I'm here because of you. So, I have
nothing but love and adoration in my heart, only for you. *(Expression)*

Peace

Thank you Lord, for this precious and holy jewel, a jewel of
peace, is just what I needed. Your peace for today; received.
(Tenderly)

Your Love

God your love comforts me; your love keeps me
sound. Your love is what turned me around.
Yes, Lord, your love did all that for me.

Yes

Yes Lord, yes Lord, yes Lord...
Yes Lord, yes Lord, yes Lord...
Repeat *(x 5)*

Shine

May the glorious light of the (son) *Jesus*, shine His face upon
you. This is my prayer for you today. Be blessed! (*Shalom*)

❖   *Love yourself as God loves you...*

Life

The wind is blowing, yes, it's blowing, and it feels like the fresh breath of
God, breathing eternal life way down into my thankful and living soul.

I Will

I will bless your name...
I will exalt your name...
I will call your name...
I will love your name...
I will carry your name...
Wherever I go Lord, wherever I go... (*Love*)

Knowing Purpose

Have you ever wondered or asked yourself, what drives you to go on with your life? Could it be, that even with new challenges we're going to face daily, we believe that there's a purpose? Knowing that alone, and not understanding every detail of Gods plan for our life is good and encouraging enough to go on with our lives. Why? Because, we trust God's purpose for our bright future! Now, that's knowing, believing and seeing purpose in action.

Hope

Hope alive is keeping hope alive in our hearts. Looking forward to embrace the new as we leave the old behind. *Hope!*

A Moment of Colors:

Have you ever thought of colors and how beautiful they are? Well, here are a few colors for your day...
Blue: In the book of *Genesis*
It says that the Lord God blew the breath of life
into the nostrils of man and woman too.
Praise God and hallelujah for blew!!!

Yellow: it doesn't really matter
Whether we yell low or we yell loud, because
God still hears us even if we choose not to yell at all.
Green: hello green. Green continues to scream life. Life that grows and flows will continue to scream like an ongoing stream. Therefore, we must thank God for the color green.

Red and orange, compliments each other just like salt and pepper. Question, does your life compliment the character of your *Heavenly Father!*

Wisdom through Colors

Buying flowers or picking paint colors, colors are known to reflect our personalities. Personalities are known to define the person. But let's make sure that the *Holy Spirit*, the real person is reflected through our inside colors.

Through

Closer to you Lord, I will find. I will press with a
new mind. I will press with perseverance.
I will push through the dark valleys, having mine eyes fixed only
on you. Yet, knowing I've already come through. *(Reassurance)*

Think Positive

How to stay positive in a negative world?
Well, that's a good question. Fight! Fight! Fight! Yes, that's it!!!
Did you think my answer was going to be different? Ephesians
6 says "We fight against spiritual, evil, and negative forces." So,
if someone makes you upset, please don't fight them. Use your
spiritual weapon "Prayer" and fight against the real enemy, (devil)
the one who's trying to mess up your day. Continue to show love
in a negative world. Now that's positive thinking. *(Devotion)*

New View

Oh, doesn't it feel good to enjoy something new? It's
like having a fresh perspective with a fresh view.

Fun

Eternal fun? Yes, heavenly host bid me to come,
around the throne of grace if I may.
Heavenly host, room to worship for eternity, I will enjoy. To
worship for all of eternity; proclaiming Holy, Holy, Holy, Holy,
Lord God Almighty. Forever and ever, amen! *(Longing)*

Your Name

How beautiful is the sound of your name dear *Jesus*, a sound
like no other. Oh, how beautiful... like a lovely song, singing
in my ears calming every one of my fears. Oh, how beautiful
is your name dear *Jesus*, how beautiful! *(Reflections)*

❖ *Another day with our Savior is the best day ever. (Rejoice)*

Rejoice (Change)

I will rejoice in your holiness,
Rejoice for change
I will choose to rejoice in your holiness because it's done
all in *Jesus* name! Hooray for change!!! *(Thankfulness)*

Cast Down!

Thinking positive is when we choose to cast down every
negative thought that comes to the door of our minds, for
us to entertain. Listen! Let us start casting them down now!
Satan, get out of my mind and my thoughts! I rebuke you in
the name of *Jesus* mighty and powerful name! *(Strength)*

Start!

Before we finish anything, we must first start. So, let me ask you a
question. Do you have something that you need to talk to our *Heavenly
Father* about? STOP! Now pause... And tell God everything, He is
here right now! Go ahead, just start the conversation now. *(Cleanse)*

How (Selah)

How wonderful, how excellent Selah!
How marvelous, how victorious Selah!
How you love me...
How creative and skillful Selah!
How patient and kind, o how you love me...
How thoughtful and compassionate Selah!
How wise and knowledgeable, o how you love me...
How forgiving and caring Selah!
O how you love me, you love me, you love me, Selah! *(Teardrop)*

Time Is Right

Sitting and waiting for my loves tender embrace, holding me tight. Lord, I'm here because the time is right. Here waiting for your wisdom to help guide me from day to night. Come dear Jesus, the time is just right, as you hold me close and tight.

Days

Days come and days go but a day with the Lord is well worth it! *(Eternal)*

Cry Out!

Cry out and praise the good Lord, o my soul!!!
Praise Him in the boisterous wind! Praise Him in every kind of tree! Lift His name, as a new flower that blossoms in the morning. Because I refuse to let a non-living rock cry out for me.

Still Love Me

Will you still love me, when I don't give you what you think you deserve...Will you? Will you love me when it seems as though, I'm so far away? Yet, knowing that we should live and walk by faith? Or, will you reach out to me and bring me closer to your loving heart... Will you? What if I flee into another's arm...Or, will you hold on to me tight with the strength of your palms? Will you still love me...I want to know? My love...Rest assured, for you will always and forever be in my heart you see. Now... will you still love me? *God*

Sin

It's another day to be cleansed and another opportunity
to live without sin, Hallelujah!!! *(Purify)*

Loves Package

Love should never be weighed or judged by mere words, love
never changes... Love is an action word, always in motion. Love
is never lazy; love is constantly working but never too busy...
Love knows when to slow down and love knows when to speed
up...Wisdom also resides in the bosom of love and knowledge
and understanding are considered to be hidden treasures
within... Love's gift, is a package deal. When we ask for love,
God gives us the whole package!
God is love! *(1 John 4:8) KJV*

Seeking

Seeking the heart of God is like no other. We seek after many
things. But, when we go deeper and seek after the things of
God, we will never lose! God will always give us better! Job
received more in his latter than his beginning. Now apply
Job's latter, in your thinking. And while you're seeking
God, think big!

I Told You

No matter where you are in life, call me and I will hear.
Yes, I am very near. I told you I'll never leave you or forsake
you, so trust me my dear child and please do not fear. Call
me, I am here and through your faith I will hear.
Love God

Rest

If you have ever worked on a job or owned your business, then you know what the word tired means. So, when business slows down, don't get angry. Maybe God is trying to give us rest, so take advantage of that time and do just that. Listen, there's always something to keep us extra busy, so go ahead, and refresh yourself in the Lord! *(Read Math. 11:28) again...*
REST...

On Your Mind

What's on your mind? How about telling God how much you love and appreciate Him? I believe He will love knowing, that He's on your mind. So, let's begin...I love you Lord, I've been waiting to tell you................. *(Fill In)*

Yell

Does anybody hear me...Yelling?
I'm going to have a...Good day!!!
I'm going to have a...Wonderful day!!!

Try It

God is giving out more fruit today
Why don't you try long suffering? *(Spirit)*

A Start

Ever felt like saying, my God, my God, why hast thou forsaken me? Well, the good thing is, He hasn't, God is here right now. Have faith in our *Creator* and begin talking to Him and He will make His presence known. Only trust and believe, at least that's a start.

Talk It

We must not be led by our emotions, keep walking by faith and say "God is with me, all is well, and it's going to be okay" Let's not just walk it...Let's talk it too!

Press!

Through the storms of life, I choose to press... I will tell my soul and spirit to...Press! I'm sure we will make it, but we must surely...*PRESS!*

Outpour

Lord, I'm empty and I need more, I need another outpour! I need more of your strength and I'm longing for more of your grace; I just need another outpour, yes, if only I can see your glorious face... I'm aware that I must live completely by my faith...Therefore, Lord please give me more, I really need another heavenly outpour! (*Selah)*

Every Season

Oh, how I need your presence...How I need your
comfort. Oh, how I need you Lord...
In the winter, fall, spring and summer... *Selah*
I need you lord, like the trees, need the soil... I need
you Lord, like the bird that needs a nest...
In desperation, my soul thirst...And only you
dear God, can quench my thirst!
I need you. *(Teardrop)*

Patiently

Patiently, longing to be near you...
Patiently, longing to be with you...
Patiently, waiting with my whole heart set aside only for
you my love... So, I will ...Worship, yes worship!
Worship only the lord... while I wait!

Abba Father

Abba Father, who art in heaven, hear my hearts cry...*Abba Father*;
I know I will continue to live and not die! Why? Because you
washed my dirty lost, little soul. That's why. *Thank you Jesus!*

Adjust

Did you adjust your thermostat? What do I mean? Well, look at it
this way...Have you been offended, hurt, or done wrong? OK...
Don't let someone else decide how they want you to feel and
adjust your thermostat. You take control of your own emotions
and adjust it and have a relaxing and peaceful day....

Move On....

Life's challenges will come, but one thing I have found out, if
you can't change it...Then Don't! Do yourself a favor, accept
it and move on, I hope this nugget of wisdom helps.

Start

Move it, move it...
Is there something that needs to be done, (positively speaking)
but you find yourself upset and frustrated about it? All we have to
do is...start completing one thing at a time, and soon it all will be
done. Remember, before it can be completed it must be started.

Tour

Purpose...Do you know yours? If your answer is no, then
first seek the Lord and be very patient until you're sure.
Because all of us has a purpose in this land as we tour.
In this I'm very sure...

Limits...?

There's a scripture in the bible *(Galatians 5:1)* That says "*Christ has
made us free*"... But should we go beyond our limit? Should we get
drunk, or cuss someone out, inflict harm to others, or be so angry
that we provoke someone else to wrath? As Christians God has given
us set limits. So, let's not go beyond our limits of freedom, and *show*
the world what freedom really is. "*Be not entangled again with the
yoke of bondage.*" Now, can we hear "An Amen" in the house?

Nothing to Lose

Surrender I must do, to surrender is for me to choose.
Surrender only to God, for I have nothing to lose. As I humbly
surrender, so I choose. My entire body, mind, and soul is
set aside only for you to use. That's what I choose.

Speak....

Speak to me Lord and make it very clear! *I need to
hear your sweet voice, guiding and directing me. Please
keep on speaking in your child's ear. (Direction)*

Piece of Art

I bought a beautiful piece of art, that's hanging on my bathroom
wall, and it says "*Live every moment, Laugh every day, and Love
beyond words*" I do not know who wrote it. But, we should enjoy
life at its fullest, have a good sense of humor, and show love
more than we say it. In short, we should "*DISPLAY IT*" because
our whole life is a wonderful piece of the *Masters* loving heart.

If I Ever

If I ever forget to ask for your forgiveness, "My sins Lord,
please forgive." If I ever forget to ask you to lead and guide me,
"Please Lord, lead and guide me." And Lord, if ever I forget
to ask for more of your strength and grace, "Please give me
more of your strength and your grace." Why? I need them in
order to be strong and endure, to finish this earthly race.

Humbled Hearts

(Heaven)

While looking ahead there were angels all around. But, there was no need to be afraid. With that said, floating in plain sight was a beautiful bronze, elegant lady angel...and a flaming horse with fire, with a manly angel quietly riding on its back. And over to each side in the green forest were bright manly angels with bright heavenly spears, brighter than any light that human eyes have ever seen.

They were all at the entrance: welcoming all to come into heaven's gate. Saying "*Hi boys and girls,* come, enjoy, have fun, yell, and scream, while enjoying your favorite flavored ice-cream. While, angels asking "what kind do you want." Then I awoke and realized this was a dream... yes, this was all in a dream. This dream all started; with an elegant lady, welcoming, *men, women, children, and babies...* Yes, this is a very clear picture of the kingdom of heaven. *(Luke 18: 15-17)* (Humility)

Positive

Hey, let's "Thank God" for another positive day and enjoy this non-negative, God-given day. Remember, it's what we speak, that's all I have to say, Yay!

❖   *Remember: When you pray...pray real hard!*

Printed in the United States
By Bookmasters